ultimate

REALiTiES

FINDING THE HEART OF EVANGELICAL BELIEF

Written for the
Universities and Colleges
Christian Fellowship
by
Robert M. Horn

Inter-Varsity Press

INTER-VARSITY PRESS
38 De Montfort Street, Leicester LE1 7GP, England

First published 1995
Reprinted 1996

ISBN 0-85110-882-2

Set in Palatino

Typeset in Great Britain by Avocet Typeset, Brill, Aylesbury, Bucks

Printed in Great Britain by Cox and Wyman Ltd, Reading, Berks

Inter-Varsity Press is the book-publishing division of the Universities and Colleges Christian Fellowship (formerly the Inter-Varsity Fellowship), a student movement linking Christian Unions in universities and colleges throughout the United Kingdom and the Republic of Ireland, and a member movement of the International Fellowship of Evangelical Students. For information about local and national activities write to UCCF, 38 De Montfort Street, Leicester LE1 7GP.

CONTENTS

PREFACE:
THE RAIN AND
THE DEW

Moses was like many of us. 'I have never been eloquent … I am slow of speech and tongue', he confessed. God replied: 'I will teach you what to say' (Exodus 4:10–12). The gift of God's teaching transformed him. Towards the end of his life he expressed his view of God's teaching and words in a song. In the second verse he prayed: 'Let my teaching ('doctrine' in some versions) fall like rain and my words descend like dew, like showers on new grass, like abundant rain on tender plants' (Deuteronomy 32:2).

God's truths, which Moses had made his own, revived him. The pictures of rain, dew and showers were powerfully evocative in a dry, dusty, desert land, where grass and tender plants could die in a day if no moisture came. That is a picture of the need every Christian and student group has for the restoring and life-sustaining impact of God's truth. According to Moses (and the whole Bible), truth and teaching are the absolute and exact opposites of dryness and lifelessness. They are in fact the antidote to dried up, parched lives. So may the truths opened up here constantly refresh and revive all who read.

The conviction behind this little book is similar – that we cannot survive without, but will steadily grow with, the central beliefs of Christianity. This book is the latest in a line of booklets and books called *Evangelical Belief*. These have been 'short explanations of the basics of the

Christian faith' as found in the Doctrinal Basis of the Universities and Colleges Christian Fellowship (UCCF). From time to time they have been revised or updated.

These pages primarily have in mind all who, around the world, are seeking to bear witness to the truth as it is in Jesus. The principles and truths apply to all Christian witness, including that of members of evangelical student groups who stand for Christ in universities and colleges. The UCCF Basis and that of the International Fellowship of Evangelical Students (IFES) are virtually identical.

Acknowledgments

To the students, theologians, ministers, lecturers, scientist, philosopher, medic, UCCF and IFES staff and others who read this manuscript, who sent in clarifications, corrections and improvements and who are totally exonerated from all blame for the remaining deficiencies – thanks.

And to Jenny Mann, who cheerfully and at the speed of light transformed illegible, multi-corrected drafts into a publishable manuscript.

But especially to the students.

1

REALITIES, ULTIMATE AND UNIVERSAL

This book has the aim of introducing core Christian beliefs. Those beliefs have saved lives, changed lives and cost lives. They have saved people from sin and its judgment for God and eternity. God has used these truths to change people in all cultures from self-centred rebels into children, friends and servants of God. And ordinary people have given their lives, in the last one hundred years most of all, to tell and spread the news of Jesus Christ as the only way to God. Some of these people, at different periods, have been students.

The core truths expounded here are powerful and life-changing. Men and women of all backgrounds have counted it a high privilege to stand for them. They were willing to risk their reputations, and even their lives, because they believed that what God has revealed in the Bible is true. All our reflection on particular truths is set against the background of these ultimate realities, these issues of life and death.

This great succession is essentially evangelical. The several previous editions of this book were all appropriately called *Evangelical Belief*. 'Evangelicalism' has a long history. It comes from the Greek word (evangel) for gospel; an evangelical is one who believes the gospel, just as an evangelist is one who proclaims it. It is not a denominational, sectional or sectarian term. It aims simply to denote the gospel, the heart and soul of New Testament Christianity.

It has been particularly prominent at certain stages of history. In the 16th-century Reformation, for example, Lutherans were called Evangelicals rather than Protestants, as they wanted to be distinctive on the gospel. In the 18th century came the 'Evangelical Awakening' through George Whitefield, the Wesley brothers and others. Again, 'evangelical' signified a return to the gospel. The term has been used in contrasting ways since then. At some periods it has been a term of abuse (only slightly more polite than fundamentalist or obscurantist). With the general decline of numbers in non-evangelical or anti-evangelical churches, it has become more accepted and respectable – and perhaps less clearly defined.

Those who call themselves evangelicals would be content to use the unadorned title of 'Christian', were it not for the fact that all sorts of widely differing views also claim that term. Some of these make no pretence to be biblical or to uphold the biblical gospel, some deny it and set it aside. For clarity of thought and action, the term seeks to focus on the biblical gospel and revelation.

Evangelicalism is therefore a blend of belief and practice, truth and experience, revelation and obedience. It is a call to practice arising out of belief, to experience flowing out of truth, and to obedience responding to revelation. It is neither abstract dogma nor a list of rules and regulations. It is to do with truth being worked out in life, through God's grace.

The gospel begins with the call to repent and believe, to turn around in our attitude to God and ourselves, to put away all that is wrong and to trust Jesus Christ. Evangelicalism comes to express the core of what God has revealed in the Bible, in order to have a profound effect on our whole life and motivation. It is as exciting as it is awesome.

This book looks at evangelical belief as it is expressed

in the doctrinal basis of both a national and an international student movement – the Universities and Colleges Christian Fellowship (UCCF) in Britain, and the International Fellowship of Evangelical Students (IFES) in over 130 countries around the world. Their bases, all but identical in wording, are the platform and inspiration for evangelism and Christian living in a range of different cultures and societies. They are in that sense universal in their acceptance and application – as we would expect from the God of truth who so loved the world. As Paul said to the Christians in Thessalonica: 'The Lord's message rang out from you … your faith in God has become known everywhere' (1 Thessalonians 1:8). Or as he wrote to the Romans: 'Your faith is being reported all over the world' (Romans 1:8). Today the 'everywhere' and the 'world' have been extended and Christian students are penetrating more and more universities with the evangel, with the core truths set out in this basis.

Some books are suggested for further study, to be consulted on any point where a more in-depth treatment is desired. Some questions are offered at the end of each chapter, for use by individuals or in groups. Chapter eight gives some suggestions on how Christian Unions can take up the truths of their doctrinal basis in their teaching meetings, study groups and evangelistic events.

This book is simply an introduction, a starter pack.

Questions
1 What is, or should be, the heart and soul of evangelicalism?
2 What is the significance of the fact that this Doctrinal Basis has worldwide acceptance?

Evangelicals: what are they?

Four of their characteristics are these:
1. Evangelicals seek to be gospel people
   They believe the evangel and seek to hold and
   to spread this good news. Evangelism is in their
   heads and their hearts.

2. Evangelicals seek to be Christ-centred people
   The gospel they believe and have experienced
   has Jesus Christ as its centre and his sacrificial
   death and physical resurrection as the basis of
   forgiveness, new life and hope. Christ is the
   focus of their thinking and devotion.

3. Evangelicals seek to be Bible-based people
   They take their understanding of the gospel, of
   Jesus himself and of all truth not from human
   opinions, but from the Bible, the Word which is
   God's authoritative revelation of himself. The
   Bible is the source of their convictions and their
   conduct.

4. Evangelicals seek to be focused people
   From the Bible they derive their priorities:
   God's authority over human ideas, God's
   gospel rather than human solutions, God's Son
   as the only way, men and women as lost and
   needing his pardon, these truths as paramount
   and unifying in relation to differences between
   Christians.

Evangelicals seek to work out the implications of these
convictions for every sphere of life – individual and
social, family and work, study and action, creation
and culture, church and society, time and eternity.

2
ON AND UP
FROM
BASE CAMP

Every Christian has opportunities and problems. Some give the impression that their lives are one long triumphal procession, a continuous mountain-top experience; others look as though they are always head-down in the valleys. The Bible has light to throw on all this.

All the characters of Old Testament history had their ups and downs, whether through hard circumstances or falling to temptations – think of Abraham and Moses, Samson and David. And the Bible gives us warnings from the sad examples of everyday people – such as the Israelites who experienced the exodus deliverance and then sinned in their desert journey (1 Corinthians 10:6, 11).

It was the same in New Testament days. To say the least, the gospel made some terrific advances through the early Christians. At the same time, some ordinary church members had a problem in believing that God had worked for Peter. They could not accept the words of the servant girl, Rhoda, when she told them that God had answered their prayers and released Peter from prison (Acts 12:15). Or think of three typical problems that James mentions in his letter: those who gave preferential treatment to the rich; those who were unbridled in the use of their tongues; and those who started quarrels because of their coveting (James 2:1–4; 3:1–2; 4:1–3).

Even the leaders had problems. Remember how

Peter failed to act 'in line with the truth of the gospel' in Antioch and had to be rebuked (Galatians 2:14). Or listen in on the 'sharp disagreement' between Paul and Barnabas over what to do about Mark, who had deserted them (Acts 15:39).

Bible characters had their wanderings and wonderings, so it is no surprise that we do too. It is easy to list some of the problems that beset believers today: problems of relationships; problems at home and at work; problems of assurance; of guidance; of prosperity or failure; of self-esteem and personal identity; problems about goals; problems of depression and loneliness; of trusting God in an age of doubt; of weaknesses … the list goes on and on.

It is often quite hard to identify what the problem is. And when we have identified the problems, the practical question is this: what do we do with them? The danger is that we become preoccupied with ourselves in ways that may simply ape society around us. The 'feel good' factor drives the content of many magazines – how I can feel good about my image, my clothes, my car, my friends, my career. Many try to offer some form of popular therapy. Some sections of the Christian world put spiritual phrases and a Christian veneer on such approaches. Hence the many books, magazines, videos, seminars and conferences that claim to speak relevantly to these matters. As Will Storrar has said, there are the 'wow' books and the 'how' books on how to deal with everything from memories to self-esteem.

This is not all to be dismissed. Much is helpful. We can all think of books or sermons that have come to our rescue on particular issues. And, of course, even a quick reading of the New Testament makes clear that it too was in business to deal with troubles and perplexities. Jesus dealt with a wide variety of problems for many different people, as the Samaritan woman and the rich young man discovered (John 4:1–42; Mark 10:17–23). Most of the New Testament's letters devote half their space to practical questions in their readers' lives and churches. The Bible faces up to such down-to-earth situations.

When we read the New Testament, however, we are left with the growing feeling that its approach is somehow different from ours. It seems to view life from another vantage point, to come to us with a radically different focus. It is not problem-orientated, though in a profound sense it is problem-solving. It is not difficulty-dominated, though it enables the disciple to overcome. It is not a 'how to' manual offering techniques, though it does give a way forward. It does not revolve around our felt needs like some counselling sessions, though it knows well enough how to handle our needs.

What is the difference between the New Testament's approach and ours? Two illustrations may throw light on this. We are like inexperienced climbers about to set out on our first expedition. Full of raw enthusiasm, we don't want to take time tediously surveying the best route to our chosen peak. It is too laborious to set up all the supplies and emergency equipment which we might need. We feel that we've got what it takes, and anyway, we want to be on our way. We have heard one or two accounts of others who made the ascent and they made it sound possible. We ignore the leader's instructions to prepare properly and set out ahead of him one bright morning.

We soon conquer a few of the foothills and feel we're making progress. Then the problems start. The mist closes in, our food runs low, we didn't pack a compass and we brought no charts. Without a base camp, the expedition will come to grief. We were too short-term in our approach, and the long-term prospects suffer.

To use a second illustration, we are like students approaching an exam. We're pressed for time and not on top of the syllabus, still less the whole subject. We become nervous and know that we need help now. So we look for quick solutions. We seek answers to fill in those gaps of which, in our ignorance, we are vaguely aware. We want someone to solve our immediate maths problem. We look up a few quotations to pad out our literature essay. By these means we may pass, but this tactic will give us no understanding or grasp of the principles of the subject. It will never make us at home in it, because it simply deals with a few random parts. It may answer for today, but will give no basis for next year. It will certainly not help us to get a job or, if we find one, to be able to keep it. It will not give us true knowledge to put into practice.

The New Testament puts things the other way round. It begins by surveying the ground and building the base camp. It stocks it with the food and equipment, maps and instructions, means of communication, emergency services and medical supplies which we will need for the ascent. Then it assures us that God himself, as the leader of the expedition, will go with us all as we climb. To take the other illustration, the New Testament starts by taking us through a lively and vital syllabus; it may not all seem relevant right now, but later on it will enable us to face and answer the questions which the examination of life will pose in each successive test. Not only that, but the Holy Spirit then commits himself to teaching and training us day by day, in the company of his people.

How does the Bible do this? Basically by introducing us to the ultimate realities. It cuts through our misconceptions and misunderstandings, brings us face to face with God and shows us how he sees things.

It presents to us the truth about God, the great overlord of our destiny. It displays his power and majesty. It describes his plans and decrees. It demonstrates that his purposes determine the world's course and our individual story, that his are the promises that count and that he has the decisive say in all that goes on. It declares, moreover, that this God is for us and that he has chosen us for good – not for any good in us, but to receive good from him.

It tells us that this God has spoken. He is not a silent deity, leaving us to guess his mind and will, but the personal God who reveals himself. He uses language, the gift he gave when he created man and woman, to tell us what he is like and what he seeks from us. His book defines the truth about ourselves. It unmasks what we are actually like, why we are as we are, what we can and cannot do, and what we are responsible for. It gives us the only totally reliable understanding of ourselves, because it sets us before our Maker.

Through the Old Testament and into the New it reveals more and more of the truth about Jesus Christ, telling us the facts about his coming in history and what those facts mean. More centrally, it shows him as the embodiment of God's unprecedented love for us. He is the one who sacrificed himself in our place, turning away the just judgment and wrath of God by accepting the penalty of our guilt. The Bible portrays him rescuing sinners of every kind – people of every class and colour, from all over the world, from every one of the hastening centuries. It reveals his eternal purpose to create a people for himself. It assures to all who trust in Christ the experience of new life and total pardon from God.

It opens up the truth about how God works in us, how he turns rebels into friends, aliens into children, lovers of self into lovers of God. The New Testament radiates the warming fact that, from the burnt-out ashes of our lives, God can reconstruct a temple in which he is happy to live. It tells how he does this by his Spirit's gentle, welcome and powerful entry into our lives. The Bible tells us that he does all this work in us within the company of his people. It stresses the fact that we walk the pilgrim way and bear our living witness along with all those who call on his name.

It is thoroughly realistic and reassuring. Lest we harbour fears about the future, it offers us a preview of the end. We may have doubts about whether we will make it to the goal of the journey, or wonder what will happen if we fall and disappoint Christ, so the Bible announces that one day the saints will go marching in to their eternal home, bloodied in the battle but unbowed. And it promises that Christ will return.

It is in the base camp of such stunning facts and truths that the Bible begins to handle our problems. Everything, as Paul told the Christians in Rome, revolves round God (Romans 11:33–36). Everything good about our life is *from God.* He is the origin, the Lord and giver of our existence, the governor of our every breath. He made us, he meets us, he reconciles us, he renews us, he rules us. There is nothing good about us that we have not received from him (1 Corinthians 4:7). We are total debtors, he is the sole donor.

Moreover, everything about our salvation is *through him.* It is by means of his Son's life and death that we are pardoned and adopted. It is by the resurrection power of his Spirit that we have life. It is by means of his Word that we know the truth and are set free. It is by his sustaining strength that we keep going. It is by his supernatural dynamic that the gospel advances. It is all through him.

Everything is also *to him* and *for him.* He designed us to live to the praise of his glory. He made us to please him and is busy remaking us to display, both now and in the coming ages, the incomparable wealth of his grace (Ephesians 1:6; 2:7). We are here for him, to serve his purposes, do his will and honour his Son each day.

God, from beginning to end – that is the perception the Bible gives us: 'For from him and through him and to him are all things. To him be the glory for ever! Amen' (Romans 11:36).

All this has a practical bearing on our lives, individual and corporate. God's base camp is stocked with all the ultimate realities – all those supplies that we will need in our tense and testing journey through life. God's teaching programme has in it all that we shall ever need to know this side of glory. All this has two powerful effects.

First, on our approach to what we are to believe. Every age throws up its own fashionable beliefs or doubts. At various times the vogue has been for doubt to be cast on the Bible, on the resurrection, miracles or judgment, on the deity of Christ or the exclusive claims of the gospel. This is why we look for and need to find truth in the midst of confusion. The chapters that follow try to open up the meaning and relevance for today of a typical statement of faith, the one used for many years by the UCCF and many other Christian bodies. It has been of great value to countless individual churches and organizations, providing a brief summary of what they stand for.

Many national churches, student movements and mission agencies around the world now use this Basis (or one with a very strong family resemblance), showing that it transcends local differences of history, culture and background. Down the years it has exerted a strong unifying influence, holding Bible believers from different traditions together. It is a summary of 'base camp', essential, core truth – not attempting to cover everything the Bible says, but highlighting those central truths that are at its heart (or were from time to time particularly attacked). It expresses, moreover, the unity in the gospel that brings believers together from various denominational backgrounds. These are the truths which, when held by the mind and heart, inspire Christians to bring Christ to others.

The other effect of this is on our personal lives. You may have questions about yourself. Maybe you've never felt that you understood who and what you are. You remain a mystery to yourself. Why do you do the things you do? Why the gulf between where you are and what you want to be? And does your life have any significance anyway? Are you just a faceless statistic in the human crowd, just a back row member of the congregation? Do you matter to anyone? Do you matter to God?

You may be anxious about assurance, low self-esteem, feeling that you are nobody special and not noticeably gifted. You are conscious of failures and weaknesses, feeling guilty about some past sins, doing your best but sometimes unsure whether you qualify to break the bread and drink the wine at the Lord's table. You believe that God is love – but is he love to you? You know that Christ died and believe that he has done his part, but are you accepted as righteous in God's sight? This lack of assurance in turn creates a problem in your witness. If you were more convinced about God for yourself, you would be more courageous about the gospel for others.

These are genuine problems, not in the least exceptional or uncommon. That is one reason why there are so many Bible verses that speak to them – for example: Do you matter? 'Cast all your anxiety on him because he cares for you' (1 Peter 5:7). Another translation could be: 'It matters to God about you.' Is assurance possible?

'If God is for us, who can be (successfully) against us? I am convinced that (nothing) … will be able to separate us from the love of God that is in Christ Jesus our Lord' (Romans 8:31, 38–39).

Those are great verses, but God gives much more powerful help than isolated texts. Those texts, marvellous in themselves, are infinitely more glorious when seen for what they are: just some of the splendid details of the vast majestic picture that God has unveiled to us in the Bible. He wants us to stand back for a while and take in the whole canvas he has painted. He wants us to absorb and admire his breathtaking plan of salvation, the grand design of our Saviour-Sovereign. He wants us (to revert to the earlier illustration) to become familiar and thrilled with all the supplies he has laid on for our expedition. We will lose out if we merely run a cursory glance over this tin of food or that compass. Christ wants us to make our own all the resources he has bequeathed to us from his pioneering journey through life and death.

As we scan through our statement of belief in the following chapters, we stand, wondering in awe, before a panorama of the immense, many-splendoured Bible picture of God and his purposes. Each chapter sets out some of God's truths which our human minds need, and some of the heavenly resources which our earthly route will require. They are not 'problem-solving' chapters, though they will answer lots of questions. They aim to give wide-angle vision. They offer a framework of biblical understanding and that in turn can enable us to see where our questions and problems fit in. They do not answer all the questions about the way, but they do set up the base camp to equip and encourage us to go higher up and further on with God. This is, after all, simply a brief introduction to core Christian beliefs.

The truths outlined in these chapters can change us from being self- or problem-centred to being God-centred. They can root out our obsession with short-term cures and set us on the road to long-term spiritual health. They can lift us from the valleys of our own (little?) troubles, to the high ground of loving God and knowing his love poured out into our hearts by his Spirit (Romans 5:5). They can settle doubts and fears and put a new spring of assurance into our step and our service.

The truths set out here have been the inheritance and delight of believers down all the centuries. They have been rediscovered in each generation – they have to be, because they get obscured by our sinful minds (which do not like them) and the devil (who hates them). They are not in the least new in themselves, though they are ever new. They have made strong, Christ-centred Christians out of weak, self-centred mortals ever since the days when they were first revealed. By God's Spirit, they still have that power – and that is exciting for us today.

Yes, there is excitement in these pages, though it is not the froth and bubble variety that recedes when the tide of events goes out, or disappears when our fun bubbles burst. It is the excitement of being appointed to the expedition, of setting out to climb the heights. It is what Paul felt when he wrote: 'But one thing I do: Forgetting what is behind and straining towards what is ahead, I press on towards the goal' (Philippians 3:13–14). The future is still future and therefore unknown, though a new part of it arrives every day. None of us has yet climbed the peaks that lie ahead, whatever we have achieved in the past. This is why we may not see at once the relevance to the expedition of everything the leader has said or supplied. We may fail entirely to see the point of this instruction or that truth.

Some information may make no sense to us at all right now; we may think, we know better. Some maps are too detailed, we think; some directions seem odd. Surely we could work out a better route? But all that he has said and provided will come into its own as we go on. When we finally arrive, we will know that all he gave was absolutely vital to our survival and well-being.

The more familiar we are with what God has revealed, the more we shall enjoy the climb and the views. The more we use what the leader has supplied, the more he will be honoured by our progress, the better will we survive and the more strength and exhilaration will we find as we walk in his steps. The more you tread the high places in company with the Son of God, the more you will look back to thank him that he set his affection on you (Deuteronomy 7:7) and that he has met 'all your needs according to his glorious riches in Christ Jesus' (Philippians 4:19).

This book, then, is about the truth of the God who 'is able to make all grace abound to you, so that in all things at all times, having all that you need, you will abound in every good work' (2 Corinthians 9:8).

Questions

1 What would you say to the argument that doctrine is dry and unrelated to life and what we need is experience?
2 What is the biblical relationship between God's revelation and our experience – or between our understanding and our living?
3 As Christians we are pulled between being self-centred (our problems) and God-centred (his will). How does his truth help us to get things right?

3

POSITIVE
HELPS

Truth is crucial for us: at least it should be, since God went to so much trouble, over so many centuries, to give us so much of it. He obviously thinks it is vital. It is astonishing that he so much wants to talk to us. We are used to a Bible, but we are not so familiar with a doctrinal basis.

A doctrinal basis is a statement of core Christian truth, a typical expression of beliefs that stand in the main line of corporate Christian confessions down the centuries. Such a statement has a positive but limited use. Positive, in that it highlights the main truths that God has revealed, so that we may know that truth and find freedom in following it; limited, in that it does not cover all the truths in the Bible and does not itself draw out the consequences of its truths for everyday living and thinking. All down the centuries, in times of evangelistic advance or theological controversy, such summaries of Christian belief – or confessions – have been needed to clarify the truth.

If you are a Christian student leader, you may never have seen any doctrinal statement before you were approached about taking responsibility in your student group. The same may apply if you are coming into responsibilities in a church which has a doctrinal or confessional statement. Such a basis may seem a strange document, stiff with abstract nouns and technical jargon. It is not easy to get into it, so we offer two versions of a doctrinal basis below.

The first is the one in the Constitution of the UCCF and the IFES and probably your CU or evangelical student group. The other has no official standing, but is simply an attempt to make the Basis a little more accessible; it tries to express the identical truths in sentences that have some flow to them. It is a little like a contemporary translation of the Bible compared to an older version – the very same truth, but in slightly more up-to-date expression. Use whichever version is clearer to you; they both mean the same.

Bearing in mind that no difference of meaning of any kind whatever is intended in the complementary version, we shall generally refer to the latter, more contemporary one, in these pages.

The Basis has an important preamble on which two comments should be made. First, it sets out *fundamental* truths, not the total truths of *Christianity*. It is not a comprehensive, all-inclusive, statement of revealed truth. All it claims is that the basic truths *include* those stated here.

Second, it seeks to represent the truths of Christianity pure and straight, not any denominational or sectional version of them. It therefore does not touch on those matters that distinguish some of Christianity's sub-groupings from each other – issues, for example, such as the mode of baptism, millennial views, attitudes to spiritual gifts or to church structures.

We turn now to look at the various areas of truth, as set out in our confession.

The doctrinal basis of the Fellowship shall be the fundamental truths of Christianity, as revealed in Holy Scripture, including:

(a) The unity of the Father, the Son and the Holy Spirit in the Godhead.

The Father, the Son and the Spirit are one in the Godhead.

(b) The sovereignty of God in creation, revelation, redemption and final judgment.

God is sovereign in creation, revelation, redemption and final judgment.

(c) The divine inspiration and infallibility of Holy Scripture as originally given and its supreme authority in all matters of faith and conduct.

The Bible is inspired by God (God-breathed) and infallible, as originally given, and is the supreme authority in all matters of what to believe and how to live.

(d) The universal sinfulness and guilt of human nature since the fall, rendering man subject to God's wrath and condemnation.

Since the fall, human nature everywhere is sinful and people are guilty; this makes everyone subject to God's wrath and condemnation.

(e) The full deity of the Lord Jesus Christ, the incarnate Son of God; his virgin birth and his real and sinless humanity; his death on

The Lord Jesus Christ is fully God, his incarnate Son; he was born of a virgin, his humanity real and sinless; he died on the cross, rose bodily the cross, his bodily resurrection and his present reign in heaven and earth.

and is now reigning in heaven and earth.

(f) Redemption from the guilt, penalty and power of sin only through the sacrificial death once and for all time of our representative and substitute, Jesus Christ, the only mediator between God and man.

We are redeemed from the guilt, penalty and power of sin only through the sacrificial death once and for all time of our representative and substitute, Jesus Christ, the only mediator between God and sinners.

(g) Justification as God's act of undeserved mercy, in which the sinner is pardoned all his sins, and accepted as righteous in God's sight, only because of the righteousness of Christ imputed to him, this justification being received by faith alone.

Sinners are pardoned all their sins, and accepted as righteous in God's sight, only because of the righteousness of Christ, credited to them; this justification is God's act of undeserved mercy, to be received solely by trust in him.

(h) The need for the Holy Spirit to make the work of Christ effective to the individual sinner, granting him repentance towards God and faith in Jesus Christ.

The Holy Spirit is needed to make the work of Christ effective to individual sinners, and enables them to turn to God from their sin and to trust in Jesus Christ.

The Basis	A complementary version
(i) The indwelling of the Holy Spirit in all those thus regenerated, producing in them an increasing likeness to Christ in character and behaviour, and empowering them for their witness in the world.	The Holy Spirit dwells in all those he has regenerated, producing in them increasing likeness to Christ in character and behaviour, and giving them power for their witness in the world.
(j) The one holy universal Church, which is the Body of Christ, and to which all true believers belong.	The one holy universal church is the Body of Christ to which all true believers belong.
(k) The future personal return of the Lord Jesus Christ, who will judge all men, executing God's just condemnation on the impenitent and receiving the redeemed to eternal glory.	The Lord Jesus will return in person, to judge everyone, to execute God's just condemnation on those who have not repented and to receive the redeemed to eternal glory.

The basis covers four major areas of truth:
1. God and his word;
2. Human need and God's rescue;
3. God's work for us and in us; and
4. Christ's people and Christ's return.

The approach in this book rests on the persuasion that the Doctrinal Basis *helps*. That word focuses on the fact that the truths in the Basis do five things:

1. *Highlight* the truths that God has revealed, the core convictions that unite God's people;
2. *Explain* the realities of life to us and give us a realistic world-view;
3. *Liberate* our minds to follow God's thoughts, delivering them from our personal preferences and society's false standards;
4. *Protect* us from error and digression; and
5. *Send* us out to live and witness for Christ, equipped with a clear message for a needy world.

First, therefore, it tells us the core of *what* God has revealed. Then the other four elements show *how* this revelation affects our lives.

Four of these five helps are clearly positive. Highlighting the central truths is like shining a light into a dark place (2 Peter 1:19). Getting the controller's explanation of what is going on in the world is stabilizing in an otherwise unsettling world. Finding freedom to open our minds and explore what is true is a great stimulus, totally different from wrestling with human speculations. And being sent out by the one who is truth and has all authority gives profound significance to our whole mission. What could be more worthwhile than to be thinking his thoughts after him and living our lives for him?

The other element, protection from error, may sound negative – but no more so than when we try to prevent infection for our physical health. Truth leads to sound health, untruth to weakness or worse. Jesus said that the Pharisees were blind guides, following merely human tradition and thus making the Word of God void (Matthew 23:16; Mark 7:13). Paul warned about 'a different gospel—which is really no gospel at all' (Galatians 1:6–9). Error is life-threatening, not merely an alternative set of ideas. And there is no reason to suppose that there is less error around today than in

New Testament times. To benefit from the wholesome intent of God's truth it is always necessary to 'keep watch and to be on our guard', as Paul urged the Ephesians (Acts 20:28–31).

A basis that is securely rooted in Scripture can help to defend a church or a student group from error on the central truths. But even that is with the aim of being positively committed to 'God and to the word of his grace, which can build us up . . .' (Acts 20:32).

Such basics have sometimes been used negatively, in a ghetto mentality, merely to mark out a group's identity and keep out trespassers. That is not the aim. At the same time, it is beyond doubt that Jesus, Paul and other New Testament writers, all stressed truth and warned about the danger of error.

So all five uses of the Basis do, in fact, have a positive aim.

Such a basis does not endorse an insecure, defensive, enclave mentality. It expresses the truths that we are to take to our hearts and pass on to those around us. The Bible itself, necessarily, has negative aspects as it talks of condemnation, lostness and judgment; but it speaks of those in order to point to the positives – the offer of forgiveness, the transformation of life, the hope of heaven.

It is similar with the Doctrinal Basis. It is not Big Brother's ruler to be used to rap dissenters over the knuckles. To the extent that it reflects the Word of God, it is a signpost not merely to correct belief, but to life.

Questions

1 Why do we need to have a doctrinal statement of our beliefs? Would it be sufficient just to 'follow Christ' or 'believe the Bible'?
2 From what dangers can these truths protect us?

4

GOD
AND
HIS WORD

We can now apply this pattern of helps to the core truths set out in the successive clauses of the Basis. The first two sections are about God. They highlight two great truths:

(a) That God is personal: he is one, the only God, one God in three persons. 'The Father, the Son and the Spirit are one in the Godhead'.

(b) That God is infinite: he is supreme, sovereign over everyone and everything. 'God is sovereign in creation, revelation, redemption and final judgment.'

This God is never interested merely in giving abstract definitions. He is a God who acts and in his actions he always reveals himself so that he may touch us and affect our lives. We will therefore look first at the ways in which these truths touch us, and then unpack what they highlight for us.

They explain the realities of life to us. They tell us what God is like – the God with whom we have to mean business. He is personal, not just a force or a power. He acts and speaks and relates. He chose to reveal himself to men and women. He has all authority and so can come to us in any time of need. Nothing is too big for him. Nothing is beyond his knowledge. Nothing, not all the dark forces of hell, can defeat him.

The Bible often explains to us the sheer power of God. Isaiah records the time in history when God had a work of judgment to do against Mount Zion and Jerusalem – his disobedient people. He did this work by using a foreign power, the king of Assyria. That king had no intention of serving God's purposes; he had in mind to 'destroy and put an end to many nations'. But God called him 'the rod of my anger and the club of my wrath'; God's power was such that all things and everyone served his designs (Isaiah 10: 5–12).

A New Testament example, the example above all others, is the crucifixion of Jesus. That deed was perpetrated 'with the help of wicked men', by the Jews whom Peter challenged at Pentecost: 'you put him to death by nailing him to the cross'. How does the Bible account for this event? By explaining who was in control: 'This man was handed over to you by God's set purpose and foreknowledge … and God raised him' (Acts 2: 23–24).

God takes sin and evil seriously, but shows his redeeming love to those who trust him. Life often seems out of control, in the hands of unjust forces or blind fate, but that is not true. Things are not what they seem in the newspapers, on TV, or in our reflections. There is only one God.

This liberates our minds and lives. Without these truths about God we would be restricted to conjuring up the best ideas we could about him. Many people do this: 'I can't believe in a God who does that, but I can accept a God who does this.' That is a fearful bondage, to be bound to my own thoughts and concepts. Because I am finite, that is a hopeless course. Much better to know the freedom of what the infinite one has revealed. We can never be free when we are at odds with God, but we certainly can when our minds and wills are in accord with his.

Thus this protects us from error. It stops us making God as we want him to be, for that would be idolatry. It holds us back from the mistaken idea that other gods may be valid. It stops us from having ideas of God that come more from our current self-centred society than from God himself. God is not the ultimate therapist, just there to massage our egos and make us feel good. He is God; it is for us to adapt and alter to fit into his will, not to try to adjust God to what we want. 'Let God be true, and every man a liar' (Romans 3:4).

So all this sends us out for him. There is only one God, so the whole world needs to hear of him. There is only one God, so our whole lives need to be lived for him, wherever we are and whatever we do. There will be a day of judgment, so people need to know of the only one able to rescue them.

This God is all in all, so believers naturally respond by praise and love, service and witness. We can't keep him to ourselves. We turn then to the two truths that these clauses highlight about God.

God is one God in three persons

The far-reaching and glorious truth about the Trinity is beyond our full grasp, but what God has revealed of himself leads us to accept it humbly and praise him. Three strands run through what the Bible teaches about this.

First, is the assertion that there is only one God. The Old Testament says: 'Hear, O Israel: The LORD our God, the LORD is one' (Deuteronomy 6:4). That is why one God is to have all our love. The New Testament confirms this: 'For there is one God' (1 Timothy 2:5).

Second, the one God exists in three distinct persons. The Old Testament has hints and foreshadowings of this, as when God said in creation: 'Let *us* make man in *our* image' (Genesis 1:26). The New Testament is explicit. Jesus' missionary mandate commands baptism 'in the name of the Father and of the Son and of the Holy Spirit' (Matthew 28:19). The typical Christian 'blessing' has the same thrust: 'The grace of the Lord Jesus Christ, and the love of God and the fellowship of the Holy Spirit' (2 Corinthians 13:14). Ananias found that a lie to the Holy Spirit was a lie to God (Acts 5:3–4). Other obvious references are 1 Corinthians 12:4–6; 1 Peter 1:2 and Jude 20, 21. The three persons of the Godhead are distinguished, but eternally exist in perfect and eternal harmony.

Third, each person is fully God. It is not that there are three Gods, nor that one person operates in three different modes; nor that the Father is God, with the Son a lesser created being; nor that Jesus was an ordinary man whom the Father adopted as his Son at his baptism. All three are fully God and each has a distinct role in the divine plans.

The Father spoke creation into being, the Son carried out those decrees and the Spirit was active, 'moving over the face of the waters' (Genesis 1:3; John 1:1–4; Genesis 1:2). The Father planned redemption and sent his Son; the Son came and achieved our salvation; and the Spirit of truth gave us new life and power (John 3:16; Ephesians 1:9–10; John 6:38; Hebrews 10:5–7; John 15:26; 3:5–8). There is eternal equality in their essential being, but subordination in role in their perfect teamwork.

The Trinity is a staggering and utterly unique truth. It sounds complex, but that is no surprise, for we are in the awesome presence of the holy one. It profoundly affects our whole lives, in ways such as these:

a. It is essential to our salvation. If Jesus were not the Son of God, he could not save us; a mere human being could not atone for sin. But if God was in Christ reconciling us to himself, then God (and not a third party) was bearing the penalty for our sin (2 Corinthians 5:19). Moreover, it is because Jesus is both human and divine that he is able to represent us before his Father.

b. It utterly transforms our view of the world. God, as the source and centre of life, is both personal and relational. He is no impersonal force or power, and he did not create us because he needed to relate to somebody. He relates within himself. He is a unity in diversity. It is this one God in Trinity who has given us one world with infinite variety, distinction and colour. One theme, one team, leading to many variations. One God, three persons, leading to many relationships. This is why all the different aspects of creation hold together in God; life is not a random collage of disjointed parts, but a unity under God. When many people's worlds are falling apart, Christians are thankful that theirs hangs together in the one-in-three.

c. This deeply affects our devotion. There is infinite food for thought, meditation, reflection, praise and prayer in this doctrine. This God is our God, pledged to us in a covenant of grace. If we set our minds to absorb the truths of even the few verses quoted here, our hearts will be stirred to wonder, love and praise.

God is supreme

'Sovereign' is a title that has lost its force in any democratic society, with ruling monarchies a thing of the past. Kings and queens today are long on pomp and short on power, so we need to rehabilitate the term when we use it of God. It means that he alone has absolute power, that he is in sole charge, that he 'does as he pleases with the powers of heaven and the peoples of the earth' (Daniel 4:35). If being able always to do exactly what you want has anything to do with happiness and freedom, God must be the happiest and freest of all beings, since he alone is able to do just that.

God is God. He is not sitting around in heaven, waiting our permission or our prayers before he can act. He does not so much intervene in human affairs, as operate in them all the time. He 'works out everything in conformity with the purpose of his will' (Ephesians 1:11); he sustains all things by his powerful word (Hebrews 1:3); in him all things hold together (Colossians 1:17) – without him, they would fall apart.

The Basis points to four of the areas in which God did what he decided to do:

In creation

He brought a world into being out of nothing merely by his 'say-so'. The myths of other religions in Old Testament times often viewed the world as coming into being by procreation, as the 'gods' had sex with other gods or humans. The God of the Bible is totally different. The created world is not divine or part of the divine, but is his artefact. It is to be respected as coming from the Creator, but not to be confused with him. He created the universe and the sexes, and he did it by his word alone: 'God said, "let there be … ", and there was' (Genesis 1:3). The fact of creation by God is clearly affirmed and is fundamental to all the teaching of the Bible, whereas the method of creation is less to the fore.

He is the first and final source of all that is (Romans 11:36). The fact of God as Creator is the ultimate reason for caring for the world he made. It is his, not ours.

In revealing himself

We will take a closer look at how God has revealed himself when we come to look at the Bible, but for the moment we need to note that God has revealed himself in two ways. First, in the universe he created he has shown his eternal power and 'God-ness', to make people aware that he exists and that they are accountable to him. It is because they have knowledge of him, but reject him, that they are without excuse (Romans 1:19–20). And, second, in his Word he has revealed more than enough of himself for human beings to know how they may be saved and live in relationship with him (2 Timothy 3:16–17).

In redeeming us

We will see more of this later too, but being 'sovereign in redeeming' means that our salvation comes totally from him, not in the least from us. It is he who has rescued us, paid the price of our deliverance and made us free men and women through his Son. If he had not acted, we would be lost. He alone is able to save (Hebrews 7:25).

In final judgment

Because he is supreme to the end, none of us can escape facing him to hear his final verdict. Every human being will have to stand before him; all will be silent, knowing their guilt (Romans 3:19). Some standing before him will be those who confessed him and bowed the knee to him in this life; from them judgment has already been lifted, since they are forgiven because of the sacrificial death of his Son. Others will only then bow the knee (Philippians 2:10), having refused to do so in this life. God alone, not human opinions, will judge everyone in justice.

This is God: 'To him be glory for ever!' (Romans 11:36). But how has he made known to us his nature and the other truths we need to know to live aright?

The third clause of the Basis gives a straightforward answer to that question: 'the Bible is inspired by God (God-breathed) and infallible, as originally given, and is the supreme authority in all matters of what to believe and how to live'.

God has revealed himself in and through holy Scripture, the Bible. If he had not done so, everyone would be left to his or her own opinion of what God is like, or of good and evil. It is not through the Bible as opposed to his Son or his Spirit, but as the only source which gives us the authoritative revelation of his Son. Christ came as the living Word of God, Scripture as the written Word of God. Christ endorsed the Bible of his day (the Old Testament) and validated the New Testament in advance, as he promised his Holy Spirit to 'remind them of everything he had said' (John 14:26). Christ himself said that he was in all the Scriptures of the Old Testament (Luke 24:27), and obviously was also the central figure in the New. God's self-disclosure in Christ is inextricably embedded in his self-revelation in the Bible; we cannot separate the two or put one against the other. There is no Christ apart from the Christ revealed in the Bible. Other concepts of Christ arise when people make themselves judge and jury as to what to believe.

The truth this clause highlights for us is that the Bible had its origin in God, who breathed it out through the distinctive personalities of the men who wrote it, so that it comes with God's lifetime guarantee of its truth and reliability (2 Timothy 3:16). It thus carries his personal authority for what we are to believe and how we are to behave.

It explains how we may know God. We get to know other people by being with them, doing things with them, watching them at work or leisure – and listening to them. If we don't listen, we can misinterpret them completely. It is precisely the same with God and the Bible. We talk to God in prayer, but true prayer rests on knowing God; to know God we must give full attention to what he has revealed of himself in the Bible.

This is a simple but crucial point. When we read the Bible, we are reading a set of ancient writings; that is one reason why we sometimes find parts of the Bible hard to grasp. At the same time, however, we are listening to the vibrant, contemporary, personal 'now' word of God. Our clause does not make this explicit, but the Spirit who 'carried along' the writers hundreds of years ago (2 Peter 1:21), today still brings the words alive so that the Bible is always the living and abiding word of God. The Bible is not merely there so that we can check our views (as we might check our journey against a train timetable); it is the living voice of God by which he actively guides us.

This liberates our minds and hearts. Clearly it can be misunderstood and needs to be properly understood. As Peter acknowledged about Paul, some things in his letters (and other parts of the Bible) 'are hard to understand' and need to be rightly interpreted (2 Peter 3:16). And the devil is in business to blind people's minds to what is obvious to those with eyes to see (2 Corinthians 4:4). But the essence of the Bible is clear beyond dispute and its core truths stand out brightly, leading us to the opposite of small or narrow minds. How can God's own thoughts do other than prompt and enlarge our own? Those who truly get into the Bible have their minds stretched and opened as never before. The Bible is like a set of windows, through each of which new vistas open up to delight, challenge and stimulate us. The Bible speaks about the whole of life and therefore gives us the freedom to investigate and enjoy all the riches of God's world.

The Bible protects us from error. This is evident from what we have seen already. If we deny or slip adrift from any of the basic markers of God's truth, we slip away from him. Peter knew that spiritually 'ignorant and unstable people' can take and use the Scriptures, but actually 'distort them to their own destruction' (2 Peter 3:16). People can twist isolated verses of the Bible to say almost anything, so it is crucial to understand it rightly. The value of a statement like this is that it holds us to the central truths, leads us away from aberrations, and focuses on the core truths which may be clearly discerned.

And the Bible sends us out. This God is a sending, missionary, good-news God, the God who sent out his Son. Through the pages of Israel's history runs the theme of Israel as a 'light for the Gentiles, that you may bring my salvation to the ends of the earth' (Isaiah 49:6). All through the New Testament runs the call of the Great Commission, Christ's call to take the gospel to all the world (Matthew 28:19–20). The Bible is a book for others, to turn disciples into messengers, to make witness instinctive in the Christian – as happened when the early disciples in Jerusalem were scattered by persecution. Instead of crawling into their shells as a frightened minority, they went everywhere engaging people in conversation with 'the word' about Jesus (Acts 8:1–4).

By 'holy Scripture' the Basis means simply the Bible, the sixty-six books that the church has received as the 'canon' (the rule or standard) down the years. Some sections of Christendom have accepted some other writings, such as the Apocrypha, but those were never accepted on the same universal basis as the sixty-six, not least because they did not carry the same self-authenticating marks as the others. Jesus himself accepted and worked from the Old Testament as the Word of God, making clear that he took what was written there to be 'what God said'. When he was in the wilderness being tempted, he took 'what is written' in the Old Testament as the voice of God; there was no higher authority with which to reject the devil's words (Matthew 4:1–11). When he was disputing with the Pharisees, he made plain that a verse from Genesis (2:24) was what the Creator said (Matthew 19:4-5). To him what Scripture said, God said. And, as we have mentioned, he authorized those who would write the New Testament after he had gone.

God spoke in the past through the prophets and has now spoken in these last days by his Son (Hebrews 1:1–2), Christ being his final word. We cannot improve on or add to that revelation. Christ is his definitive word, conclusive for all generations. There will be no more new truth to be revealed or believed this side of glory. What God has given is more than sufficient for all we need to know until we see him face to face.

'Divine inspiration' refers to the origin of the Bible. Each book had its origin, in an obvious sense, from its human author. David wrote psalms and Paul wrote letters. Nothing must obscure the fact that all the parts of the Bible came from human writers and they all bear the marks of their individual personalities and backgrounds. Peter says matter-of-factly: 'Our dear brother Paul wrote to you …' (2 Peter 3:15) and then puts these writings alongside the Old Testament as 'Scripture'.

At the same time the words of the Bible were 'God-breathed' (2 Timothy 3:16). It is a case of both/and. Both human pens and God's Spirit were at work. Not humans imposing limits on God through their language, ignorance or prejudice, but God so supervising the whole venture that he prepared these human writers, ordered their backgrounds and experiences, set them at their particular junctures of history, so that they were able to write exactly what he wanted. No trampling on their personalities, no restrictions on his revelation, no hint of treating them like machines or robots. Some clearly state (like Luke 1:1–4) that they 'carefully investigated everything' and did their research. Some used obvious literary devices, such as acrostics. All used terms from their distinctive cultures and background. So we have fully human books from their authors, which come from the mouth of God. Maybe it is in some respects parallel to the one person, Jesus Christ: fully human, fully divine.

This is the 'divine inspiration' of the Bible. It does not mean 'inspired' in the everyday sense in which we use it, as in 'that music inspired me' or 'he scored an inspired goal at football today'. It simply means 'God-breathed'. What Scripture says, God says.

Now we seem to be in a difficulty at this point: we are quoting the Bible to prove the Bible. Is that not cheating? Surely such circular argument is a spoof proof? If I were accused of dishonest financial dealings, it would be no defence for me to stand up in court and try to prove my honesty from the letters I had written about my own character. That would be a circular or same-level argument and would be inadmissible. The only evidence that might count would be letters from my chief, from some higher or independent witness. But who is going to be the higher authority to corroborate God's testimony? God, by definition, is unique. None is his equal, never mind his superior. We can find that his testimony about himself is consistent with life and reality (that's only what we should expect). But a circular or same-level argument, totally out of court at my level, is totally fitting in respect of God. Only he can reveal himself; we can only receive gratefully what he reveals – as in the case of Jesus on earth. Jesus did not depend on others' testimony about him; they, like the Pharisees, were quite capable of letting their prejudices blind them. He simply presented himself as he was. That was self-authenticating to those who had eyes to see.

What God breathed was words. Not isolated words, but words forming phrases, sentences, paragraphs, narratives, arguments, books. Words in contexts, in the flow of an explanation or a parable. These words are his personal revelation to us. Words are overwhelmingly important. Think how crucial they are to you when you fall in love. At that point you scour your mind for the right things to say, the right propositions to convey your feelings. The urge to speak, to express your mind and heart, is irresistible. You dare not risk being misunderstood, because you want to get to the proposal. Without propositions, you could show your love in action, but that could still leave your exact desires and intentions unclear. You have to declare love in words. A wordless, unpropositional love affair is more at the level of animals than of humans.

Now some try to make a distinction between personal encounter and propositional revelation. The one is good, the other bad. The one is what we should seek – to meet God. The other is just words and abstract, more dead than alive. But all personal relationships (and true encounters with God) give the lie to this. A God who does not declare his mind in words (and deeds as well, of course) is hiding, not revealing his person. He would be leaving us to guess and speculate – and that would be cruel to us, not kind. The God of the Bible, by contrast, is gracious and not silent; he is the personal God who cares enough to speak words.

All God's deeds in history need to be explained in words. Many tribes wandered from place to place at different periods of Old Testament history, so there was nothing unique about the mere wanderings of the Israelites. What turned those events into revelation of

God and his ways was that he spoke about them. He gave his divine 'running commentary', thus enabling later generations to grasp the significance of what he did. Events without words are like a television drama with the sound turned off: plenty of action, but no plot or sense. It was similar with the cross: that event would have looked like sheer tragedy and victimization if God had not given us so much explanation in words in the Bible.

This all follows from God breathing out the Bible. If that is its origin, what kind of a book is it? One that can only be described by a term such as 'infallible'. This word has been disputed very often, by critics and sometimes by friends, as has every word which has been proposed to convey the same meaning – entirely trustworthy, reliable, true. The point of trying to find the words to describe the nature of the Bible is, however, just this: if the Bible is God-breathed, then the Bible shares the qualities and characteristics of its author. Anything I write carries my characteristics – fallible, liable to be mistaken, partially right, partially wrong, etc. Anything God says, by contrast, is totally true, secure, non-misleading, without mistake … infallible. So what all these words are trying to convey is that the Bible has its divine author's characteristics. Infallible may or may not be the best word for God in every context; it has different overtones to different people. The basis of the International Fellowship of Evangelical Students, seeking to make exactly the same point, uses 'entirely trustworthy'. But it is beyond doubt that God is true, does not mislead, conveys no errors and can be wholly relied on. That is the intent of the term here, to say that the Bible is his book.

This is no late 20th-century invention, either. Evangelicals today inherit the term 'infallible' from, for example, the famous and widely influential 'Westminster Confession of Faith' of 1644, which talked of 'the infallible truth and divine authority of the Bible'.

The 16th-century reformers like Cranmer, Ridley and Jewel, in turn follow on from medieval theologians like John Wycliffe, who called the Bible 'the infallible rule of truth'. Then the line reaches back to Augustine, bishop in North Africa in the 5th century, who wrote that Scripture 'can neither err nor deceive' (*nescit falli nec fallere*). And they all rested their case on our Lord's view of the Old Testament, at which we glanced earlier in this chapter.

'Infallible' is not an abstract concept, but a way of stating the qualitative difference between Scripture as the Word of God and all other sources of knowledge. It means that, if Scripture comes into conflict with any other writing, then the other must give way and Scripture must teach us and rule. It is the final arbiter.

This infallible Word needs to be interpreted properly. More or less anything can be 'proved' by wresting verses out of context, and many who believe in the Bible are very bad interpreters of it, imposing their personal, denominational or cultural prejudices on it. The Bible consists of many different types of writing, from historical accounts to poetry, from parable to apocalyptic, from prophecy to songs. Each must be taken for what it is, so that the Bible's mix of divine acts in history and divine explanations of the events is held together. The doctrinal basis is a help here in focusing on the main stream of God's revelation. Obviously, God does not either endorse the devil's words as recorded in the Bible, or approve the arguments of Job's comforters. But in the context of the overall narrative, and in a book often written in idiom for popular understanding, all the components take their place and make sense. The result is a unified whole. It is because there is a consensus about truth in the Bible that we today, and Christians down the ages, have been able to have clear doctrinal statements.

People have tried to rubbish the Bible by pointing out that it often uses the language of appearances. It talks of the rising and setting of the sun, but then we still do so in a scientific age. It does not teach an outdated cosmology. When Paul wrote of 'in heaven and on earth and under the earth' (Philippians 2:10), he was quoting a hymn and using a phrase that is a fine poetic way of saying 'every being'. He was not teaching or believing in a three-decker universe, as some try to assert.

Because the Bible is an infallible guide, our concern is always with the intended sense of the passage – what it means, not with what it could be made to say, but what God purposed to say in it.

Taking the Bible as trustworthy simply means receiving all that it teaches and affirms. It may be found not to teach some things that we have been told it does; we may find that our backgrounds put blinkers on our eyes and prevent us from seeing its meaning as we should. This is one reason why the Bible will go on surprising us all our life long. We will often say: 'How did I miss that for so long? How come I didn't see that before?' We don't always see what stares us in the face.

This nature of the Bible leaves us with the responsibility rightly to interpret the God-given Word. We can take up that task, assured that God has given us a clear word, and that he wants us to arrive at an understanding of what he has said – especially on such core truths as the Basis enshrines. That assurance also rests on two other facts: one is that God has given us his Holy Spirit to help our understanding and obedience. We obviously want to appeal to the original author to help us see what he meant; and the Spirit willingly gives his help when we ask him – help that may come directly to our minds as we pray and ponder the text, or through preachers or through Bible guides and commentaries.

The other is that he gave his book to us together. It is the family Bible, the revelation that belongs to the whole people of God. Understanding it is a communal task. This would have been a fact of life in the early church: when one of Paul's letters arrived, they would all have sat round to hear it read and to interpret it together. Bible study groups are important, alongside personal Bible study.

'As originally given' is meant quietly to make the point that when Jesus, Paul and others refer to what is written, they refer to it as it was given – rather than to copies or translations of the original writings. Excellent as many versions are, we do not mistake them for the originals, which came out of situations like this: 'These things happened to them as examples and were written down as warnings for us' (1 Corinthians 10:11).

We do not have autograph copies of the original manuscripts, but biblical scholarship is aiming all the time to get as near as it can. We are more than close enough to them to know that the original meaning is not in doubt. The few details that remain unresolved in no way affect the sense. It is worth pointing out that it is precisely because scholars (of all persuasions) believe that there were originals, that they devote so much painstaking effort to establishing the original wording as the basis for all textual criticism and for accurate modern versions.

'As originally given' points to the facts that no copyist or translator has ever been perfect and that the first manuscripts have not survived. The phrase commits us to being open always to possible improvements in text and translation, in the light of further discoveries. We do not canonize any one translation, as the Catholic church did for centuries with the Latin Vulgate.

In fact, the Hebrew and Greek texts are amazingly preserved, so that no crucial point of teaching is in any doubt. In any case, the scrutiny of Hebrew and Greek texts and the science of Bible translation are highly developed disciplines. And we can be sure that God meant his word to be translated without distortion; that was what his Spirit was doing on the day of Pentecost, when they 'each heard in their own native language' (Acts 2:6, 8, 11). We can both believe in the text as originally given, and accept the versions we have as fully reliable in what they teach.

All this means that the Bible comes to us with God's stamp of approval. It has authority because it is *his* voice. He supremely has the right to rule over our lives and his product, the Bible, carries his supreme authority. 'Supreme' means that the Bible has the final and decisive say. Church tradition and history can teach us a lot; human reason can have valid insights; spiritual intuition can have an influence on us. But what the Bible says is what settles any matter of what to believe or how to live. All those other 'authorities' can err and mislead; only the Bible is always true in what it means to say. This is why it alone can bring God's rule into our lives; it has that practical purpose, so that we end up preserved from attractive errors, and obey God, not just debate about him.

This authority covers ... life. Life is one and indivisible, which is why we are to love God with all our heart, soul, mind and strength (Mark 12:29–31). What we believe in our minds is bound up with how we live, the values we hold, the way we spend our time and the priorities we have. The Bible thus is God's authority over our whole existence – from the convictions we adopt to the conduct we pursue. We dare not accept the

Bible's world-view and ignore its practical implications; neither may we think we can succeed in
following the Bible's ethical code while dismissing the
framework of belief from which it springs.

The Bible is an amazing book, absolutely unique
because God has given it. This is backed up by the
evidence, running through all the centuries and all
parts of the world, of lives and societies that God has
transformed through its teaching. It must be quite a
book to produce so much self-sacrifice in self-centred
human beings.

Questions

1 What are the implications of the belief that there is
   only one God – as revealed in the Bible?
2 How does the doctrine of the Trinity affect our
   Christian life? How should it, for example, affect our
   praying?
3 In what areas of our lives are we liable to ignore (or
   reject) the authority of the Bible?
4 What is the connection between the Bible and God
   speaking today?

5

HUMAN NEED
AND
GOD'S RESCUE

You would think that we ought to be able to understand human nature: after all, there is enough of it around us and in us to observe and analyse. We may not be able to fathom the infinite God, but surely we can get to the bottom of human nature on our own. Right? Wrong!

Human nature is what we see every day on our TV screens, in our student residences, in the work place, in our homes. Countless writers, artists, thinkers, teachers, psychiatrists, social workers, parents … and even politicians … have offered shrewd and true insights. Yet people constantly fail to put the whole picture together. Many theories have placed the undoubted trouble with human nature outside the person, claiming that people are essentially good, but that the problem comes from housing conditions, poverty, lack of education, etc. Others place it inside the person: in some aspect of the psyche, of some neurosis or the legacy of some abuse. The prescriptions arising from all these diagnoses are singularly ineffective. The continuing civil wars and other conflicts around the world have exploded the myths of inherent goodness or self-help.

Before we unpack what is wrong with human nature we need to recall the fact of God as Creator. He made human beings in his image. They are a 'ruined temple' now, but were once a beautiful and 'very good' one.

The Christian understanding of creation explains the greatness of human nature, its capacity for courage, bravery and sacrifice: its abilities to create great art, compose great music, think great thoughts and be continually inventive. The great sculptors, painters, composers, physicists, engineers, space scientists, writers and explorers all use gifts which God has put into human beings, even though many do not acknowledge their source. All this comes from being made in God's image: signs of that image are still visible, even amid its ruin.

It is striking that non-Christians have difficulty in finding reason to value all individuals, classes and races equally. Everyone accepts the United Nations' *Declaration of Human Rights*, but it is not easy to find a non-Christian basis for it. It is only in the Bible that we find such a reason and basis: that all are made in the image of God (James 3:9).

It is only God who highlights for us the full truth about people: who and what we are, what has gone wrong and what can put it right. The fourth clause of our Basis puts its finger explicitly on the problem, and implicitly raises the truth about our origin, nature and destiny as humans: 'Since the fall, human nature everywhere is sinful and people are guilty; this makes everyone subject to God's wrath and condemnation.'

It highlights the fact of a 'fall' – or, perhaps a better way of stating it, a mutiny or insurrection against God. Man and woman were created like God (in his image, Genesis 1:27), to be able to relate to him – to talk and listen, to love and be loved, to receive and share, to follow and obey. But out of misguided self-interest they threw that away and rebelled, jettisoning any prospect of continued intimacy and fulfilment; instead, they came under judgment. That is the truth of human nature ever since. The true heart of sin is rebellion and we are

49

naturally inclined to 'go our own way' (Isaiah 53:6).

This explains what is wrong with the world. The essence of our rebellion is our self-centredness. Everybody is primarily self- rather than God-centred: everyone is guilty of squeezing out the true God and setting themselves up as God in their own lives. We all 'play God' to ourselves: we make the decisions about right and wrong, about how we spend our lives, and what we think will bring us happiness. We are guilty of usurping the place that God alone deserves, and the fact that we constantly want to do that shows that we are sinful, self-absorbed.

This truth liberates us from false expectations of ourselves and society. We are freed from the 'quick fix' approach to problems, whether social, economic, psychological or spiritual. The trouble is deep inside and needs radical, long-term treatment. No experience, formula or technique can offer an instant way out. It is a great relief to be biblically realistic at this point, not least when many in the religious world become oppressive with their wonder cures.

At the same time this liberates us to have confidence that the God who made us knows how to bring us through; that his Spirit will be steadily working to renew us from the inside out, helping us to grow more like him each day and each year.

This revelation about humans also protects us from pride and smugness. We are all prone to boost our own egos, to think of ourselves more highly than we ought. This truth tells me the facts, not just about the world at large, but about myself in particular. *I* am inherently sinful and guilty: if there is anything good about me, it is only because God has done it. We need protection from the pervasive sin of pride. This truth forewarns us that our sinfulness can surface distressingly at any time. We shall be perfect only in the life to come.

This also sends us out. What people need is to be delivered from themselves, from the self-twist of their natures and all its consequences in their lives, now and in the world to come. People do not have to go on in lostness, alienation and condemnation: they can come to God. This truth is a potent stimulus to evangelism and to simply caring for others.

The truth that this clause expresses is pivotal for life and eternity. The human race is not gradually moving upwards on some cosmic moral escalator. Humans rebelled and turned their backs on God. This has affected our whole character. We are not as bad as we could be, but every part of us is penetrated by sin or self-love – our minds, memories, wills, consciences, thoughts, words, deeds, relationships, etc. Our motives are never 100% pure. We may or may not suffer from guilt feelings, but we are objectively guilty before God. We cannot come to him unless and until that guilt is removed.

This is why we are subject to 'God's wrath and condemnation'. God's anger is pure and perfect, absolutely justified and entirely free of evil or vindictiveness. It is simply his holiness responding to arrogance and wrong (Romans 1:18ff). God gave us our chance and we wilfully blew it. How can he not be displeased? Sin is moral and cosmic vandalism, smashing up what God gave for our pleasure. It is as though we were given the freedom of a vast estate, but then – instead of enjoying it – went round removing the signposts, tearing up the fences and knocking down the buildings. We should be angry at sin's trail of evil and destruction; how can it be less offensive to the holy Creator of it all?

The staggering truth, however, is that God did not let his wrath run on. To the very people who had rejected his rule and incurred his judgment he sent his Son, his one and only. Here is love, vast as the ocean …. Here is love in action, God himself, coming as the Son, taking human flesh and becoming fully human in order to turn away from us his own proper wrath on humanity. Here is the role reversal of all time. On the one hand, earth for the one from glory and death for the one who is life. On the other, heaven for the condemned and resurrection for the dead. The innocent was murdered while the guilty ran free.

So the next two clauses highlight for us who Jesus is and what he came to do: 'The Lord Jesus Christ is fully God, his incarnate Son: he was born of a virgin, his humanity real and sinless: he died on the cross, rose bodily and is now reigning in heaven and earth.' 'We are redeemed from the guilt, penalty and power of sin only through the sacrificial death once and for all time of our representative and substitute, Jesus Christ, the only mediator between God and sinners.'

These clauses explain to us the person of Christ, why he came and what God is doing in history. We need such an explanation, for a virgin birth and a resurrection are not part of everyday experience. Many have doubted them in the case of Jesus, not for lack of evidence, but because they were one-offs, not susceptible to scientific testing by repetition. He, however, was unique.

We urgently need a true explanation of Jesus. It is unthinkable to conclude that he was mad, suffering from delusions of grandeur. It is implausible to think him bad, trying to con people with his claims to deity. Also, it is impossible to classify him merely as good, in the light of his claims. The evidence drives us to conclude that he was God come in the flesh. He stands there, the one totally unique figure of all history, the only perfect and sinless human being, making staggering claims to be God and displaying the most self-sacrificing love the world has ever seen. We dare not ignore him, but how we 'explain' Jesus depends on our starting-point.

If we say that the supernatural cannot occur, then obviously there could be no virgin birth or resurrection: if they could not happen, then they did not. That is to shut the mind to a possible explanation before looking at the evidence. If, by contrast, we allow that the supernatural could occur, then it all fits. It is not in the least surprising that no less a person than the eternal Son of God should enter humanity by virgin birth and leave the grave by resurrection. It is not in the least surprising that he was raised; the shock would have been if death could have held the one who had the power of endless life (Acts 2:24). That is the only conceivable outcome for one who was not mad or bad, but God as a human being in a human body.

As such, Jesus is liberation itself. All of us as human beings want to be free. We feel instinctively that freedom will come only as we break with authority and do our own thing. So we look for space to be ourselves, away from the constraints of others. Paradoxically, however, the only truly free people are those who are the servants or slaves of Jesus. To serve him is to enjoy perfect freedom. To serve him is to be in touch with the one who gives meaning to life, to be in line with what God meant us to be. True freedom has at its centre this amazing person, who calls us friends and gives us our dignity and personhood.

This Jesus also protects us from going astray. If we are right about him, we will have the right orientation about everything else. We will be preserved from thinking that there is any other way to God apart from him. He, rather than any offered spiritual experiences, will be central in our Christian lives. The Spirit will be seen as focusing on Christ, not himself.

And he will send us out. After all, he gave the 'everyone must go' command in his great commission. 'As the Father has sent me, I am sending you' (John

20:21). As he was sent, so he sends us. We are witnesses to who he is and what he has done and can do. The heart that does not want to make him known has never met the Son of God.

So what precisely are the truths highlighted about Jesus? He is at once fully God and fully human 'in the flesh' (incarnate). He was not the latest improved-model human, with a higher moral specification than the rest of us. He was altogether 'other' in his perfection, yet able altogether to identify with us in our humanity. He had full deity and came (from his divine pre-existence) into this world, conceived super-naturally by the Holy Spirit, without a human father's intervention, and born naturally to his human mother, Mary (Matthew 1:18, 20, 23; Luke 1:34–35). He was one person, at the same time divine and human. That is why prayer should be directed to *him*.

His humanity was totally genuine. He knew the human experiences of homelessness and hunger (Matthew 8:20; 25:35). He felt the human emotions of joy and sorrow (even tears), of anger and compassion (Luke 10:21; John 11:33–35; Mark 3:5; Matthew 9:36). He was genuinely tempted (Matthew 4:1). He plainly enjoyed human friends (Luke 15:1–2), and yet at times was left totally alone (Matthew 26:56).

He left glory, the environment of deity, laid aside his majesty and came incognito. Who, after all, would look for or recognize God on the gallows? But there he was, until he rose and ascended, to be crowned with glory and honour as the ruler ('Lord') of heaven and earth. The clause speaks of Christ's 'present reign in heaven and earth'. What this does not mean is that now, on earth, everything is running according to God's ideal moral order. Holiness and love, goodness and well-being obviously do not have the field to themselves at the moment; sin is clearly not yet banished and gone.

Death and mourning, crying and pain are still part of 'the old order of things' in which we now live (Revelation 21:4). The whole creation is groaning right up to this present time, as we wait eagerly for the redemption of our bodies (Romans 8:22-23).

But the crucial question is: who is in control? It is not a balanced contest between God and the devil (dualism), even though the latter is still blinding eyes to the gospel (2 Corinthians 4:4). All authority in heaven and on earth has been given to Christ (Matthew 28:18). His plan is moving to its climax. The cross was the decisive battle, the resurrection the turning point; now he is pursuing his mopping-up operations until he has put all his enemies under his feet, the last enemy being death (1 Corinthians 15:25–26). He is in such complete control that he can and will choose the moment to return. He is now head over all things for the church (Colossians 1:18). There is only one absolute ruler in the universe.

The 'present reign of Christ on earth' does not mean that we can claim to have heaven fully here and now; God can do anything he pleases, but earth is earth and heaven is heaven. Earth is not heaven, but Christ is reigning. We pray that his kingship will come more and more, because we want an end to all that offends him. One day he will 'begin to reign' in the absolute and total sense, when there will be no more sin or death (Revelation 11:15, 17). Meanwhile, we live in hope. 'At present we do not see everything subject to him. But we see Jesus ... now crowned with glory and honour' (Hebrews 2:9).

What Jesus came to do is summarized in the term 'redemption'. To redeem means to deliver, release or set free, and to do so by facing and accepting whatever cost is involved. Jesus faced the need for a 'sacrificial death', knowing that we could not be liberated from our guilt unless he accepted the death penalty due to us. This is why he became a curse for us (Galatians 3:13).

The Bible itself gives us many angles on the death of Jesus. It is an example (1 Peter 2:21); it secures reconciliation (2 Corinthians 5:18); it is a victory (Colossians 2:15); and it turns away the wrath of God (Romans 3:25). It means 'ransomed, healed, restored, forgiven'.

But the understanding of the death of Christ that holds all these angles together is here in the clause: redemption through the death as a sacrifice of a representative and substitute (1 Peter 2:22–24).

Sometimes we are inclined simply to be content with saying: 'Jesus died because he loved me'. To wrestle with 'theories of the atonement' seems hard, pointless and very abstract. But we could not be more wrong. If we do not grasp something of how the cross relates to our need and secures our salvation, we will not be able to answer the devil's accusations (who are you to think you're accepted?), or our own doubts (I know I'm not good enough). Then our assurance of salvation and our witness are undermined. Our assurance before God is directly related to our understanding of what happened on the cross. God has gone to great pains to show us how the cross saves. He has shown us our predicament (guilty and under wrath). He has shown us that we cannot rescue ourselves. And he shows us how Christ gets us out of that pit – how he takes our guilt and removes it by his sacrificial death.

A sacrificial death means an intended, chosen death, not death as an accident or as a hapless victim. God sent his Son to be a sin offering (Romans 8:3). It means a death that is in some way related to the holy character and requirement of God.

For him to die as a representative meant that Christ was on the cross, not for any sins of his own, but to act in our interests. As Adam represented or headed up those who follow his rebellion, so Christ represents or heads up those who trust him (Romans 5:12; 1 Corinthians 15:45, 47). We were not put to death on the cross, but Christ represented us there: we are not yet in heaven, but he represents us there. He is like an ambassador for us.

A substitute is a stand-in. A rather trivial example comes from many team sports: one player may come off during the course of a game and a substitute will take his place. A more serious example comes from the terrifying sphere of hostage-taking. A courageous person could offer to be the substitute hostage, so as to secure the release of the women and children. He puts himself in their place. Jesus took our place in death. We were under sentence, deserving to die. He came down to be our substitute, to stand in our place under God's judgment, so that we could go free. This is how he gave his life as a ransom for many and bore our sins in his body on the cross (Mark 10:45; 1 Peter 2:24).

Jesus did this freely, under no coercion. It was part of the Trinity's plan of rescue, drawn up before time began, in which Father, Son and Spirit all worked as one (Hebrews 9:14). John Stott has written: 'Substitution is not a "theory of the atonement" … It is rather the heart of the atonement … The better people understand the glory of the divine substitution, the easier it will be to trust the substitute!' (*The Cross of Christ*, IVP, pp. 202–203).

It is because of this that Jesus is the only mediator between sinners and God. As fully human, he can represent and act for men and women: he can, as it were, hold our hands. As fully God, he also holds the hand of the Father. He alone, by taking our condemnation, can put our hand into the hand of God and welcome us into his family. There was no other good or great enough to pay the price of sin. No other mediator can do that – no priest, no saint, no guru, no teacher, no scholar. They all have their own account to settle with God. Only Jesus can (and did) settle ours, and he settled it once and for all (1 Peter 3:18).

The focus of the New Testament is emphatically on the cross. But that means that the focus is on the one who died on the cross. The one who died there was the one born in Bethlehem; the one born there was the one destined for the cross. The work he did and the person he was belong together. He was who he was precisely in order to do what he did.

Armed with the Bible's explanation of the death of Christ, we can face and rebuke the devil and all doubts. Christ did it, not I. He answered for me. He settled the charges against me. To any accuser we can say: put your accusation to him, he is my representative and proxy. This is hugely liberating.

> Upon a life I did not live,
> Upon a death I did not die,
> Another's life, another's death
> I stake my whole eternity.

This truth protects me against pride and self-righteousness and sends me out to say to others: 'I'm not telling you about me – I'm no better than you. But I would like to tell you about him: he's able to rescue you as well.'

So Jesus deals with our guilt and pays our penalty. It is also part of his work on the cross to deal with the power of sin. What Jesus did when he died is one comprehensive work to settle the whole question of sin and evil. Sin held power over us because it shuts us in the condemned cell and throws away the key. That bred in us a hopelessness, a sense that sinning is unavoidable.

But Christ has the key; when he releases us from condemnation, he brings us out to a new environment, a new companion and a new life style. The environment is that of access to God and fellowship with his people; the companion is the Holy Spirit, who comes to indwell us; and the life style is that of obedience to his directions.

This profoundly affects the power of sin in and over us. We are not yet in heaven, where the power of sin will not even be a memory; we are still on earth, in the arena of temptation and weakness. But Christ's cross and empty tomb have broken the power of sin and we can live with resurrection power to help us in our times of need and failure. The directions he gives us in his Word give us strength to go on with him.

The next question is this: how may we come to enjoy all that Christ won on the cross?

Questions

1 How can we use the Bible's realism about human nature to show others that God's revelation fits the observed facts of life?

2 How do popular ideas of 'sin' compare with the Bible's view? How can we communicate the latter?

3 Why is belief in the virgin birth important? What is the connection between Bethlehem and Calvary?

4 Look up the references to the emotions of Jesus (p. 54); what do they show of his humanity? And what implications do they have for our being human?

5 Why are the biblical 'theories of the atonement' so important? Where would Christian devotion be without them?

6 How can we communicate the idea of 'redemption' or 'substitution' today?

7 What is liable to happen when CUs or churches cease to be cross-centred?

GOD'S WORK FOR US AND IN US

How does all that we have been seeing become our experience? We could read it through and still feel like a spectator; how can we take part? The next three clauses sum up how God's master plan for rescue becomes personal for us. These clauses face two major issues: one concerns where we stand before God – our position or status. We are guilty. We are in the dock, accused, under sentence and awaiting our fate. The stay of execution is only temporary, for after death comes judgment (Hebrews 9:27). The other concerns what we are before God – our character or state. We are sinful, self-centred, against God by disposition and choice. We are radically unlike the holy God we face.

So we need a solution that deals with both these factors – where we are (in the dock) and what we are (compulsive sinners). If we are to know God personally, we need to have our guilt dealt with. Something must be done about the charges against us: they cannot be ignored without God becoming party to our sin. And something must be done about the way we are. Our chief sin has been in constantly flouting the chief commandment (Matthew 22:37–38); we have never, for a moment, loved God with all our being, but have persistently loved ourselves.

That state of affairs cannot go on; in short, we must be changed, so that at last we begin to love, serve and rejoice in God. These are the areas covered in these three clauses: 'Sinners are pardoned all their sins, and accepted as righteous in God's sight, only because of the righteousness of Christ, credited to them; this justification is God's act of undeserved mercy, to be received solely by trust in him.' 'The Holy Spirit is needed to make the work of Christ effective to individual sinners, and enables them to turn to God from their sin and to trust in Jesus Christ.' 'The Holy Spirit dwells in all those he has regenerated, producing in them increasing likeness to Christ in character and behaviour, and giving them power for their witness in the world.'

These three amazing clauses highlight what God has done for us (acquitting or justifying us), and what he is doing in us (by his Holy Spirit sanctifying or making us like him). We don't use these terms in everyday conversation, but we should not be surprised if these out-of-this-world realities have their own vocabulary. Every other sphere of activity has its technical terms, from sports to computers. These two terms, justify and sanctify, are simply the Bible's handy ways of compressing into single words a mind-blowing event and a lifelong process.

God justifies sinners in an instant. He pardons them, acquitting them and announcing that they may go free. He absolves them of their guilt and declares them to be accepted in his sight as if they had never sinned – as if, in fact, they were his own Son. In so doing, God is acting as a judge in a court of law. And the reason he can acquit the guilty is not by turning a blind eye, but by accepting that his Son paid the death penalty that was due to them. The price is paid, so that God both is, and is demonstrated to be, just and holy; and the sinner is welcomed into God's family, so that God is, and is shown to be, the one who justifies the ungodly who believe in Jesus (Romans 3:26).

Substitution is the basis, trust in Jesus is the key. Trust in effect says: 'I can never gain acquittal – it is all up to him. I stand condemned. All I can do is cry: "God, have mercy on me, a sinner"' (Luke 18:13). We are justified solely by faith; faith is credited to us as righteousness – faith, not our deeds (Romans 4:5; 5:1).

When God justifies a sinner, he credits his righteousness to the sinner's account. Paul begins his great treatment of justification in Romans by saying that he is proud of the gospel, for it is God's power for salvation for one specific reason – that in it 'a righteousness from God is revealed' (Romans 1:17). It is as if someone to whom you are in debt sees your depressing student overdraft and pays in more than enough to see you back in the black – permanently! – and able to start life afresh on the basis of being in credit. God similarly credits Christ's perfection to us. Instead of looking at our abysmal record, God looks at Christ's perfect record – he looks at him and, for his sake, pardons us. When Jesus cried, 'It is finished' on the cross (John 19:30), it meant that he put the 'paid' or 'cancelled' stamp across our debts.

We can sum up justification like this. When God justifies it means more than bare acquittal. As Handley Moule wrote: 'We need the voice which says, not merely, "you may go; you are let off your penalty"; but "you may come; you are welcomed into my love".' Justification deals with past, present and future – with all our sins for the duration of eternity.

It includes pardon, for God forgives and covers *the past*. Our account is settled. God cancels our debt and puts his righteousness down to our name. We have no past record to answer for when God has justified.

Justification covers *the present*, for it gives peace with and access to God and leads to adoption into God's family (Romans 5:1; Galatians 4:5, 6). God gives us his authority to call ourselves his children now (John 1:12; 1 John 3:2).

It also covers *the future*. It assures us that when all our life is exposed at the day of judgment, God's verdict of 'justified' will still stand. It brings us the last day's verdict now. It gives us immunity at the bar of God because of Christ. It promises that, having been joint heirs with him, we shall then inherit the full riches of glory (Romans 8:17). Christ paid the penalty for our sins and that penalty will never be due a second time, from us. What he did is unrepeatable, irreversible, enough.

This has unbelievable repercussions for our actual security in God; and our sense of security, of being unconditionally and totally accepted, will grow as we appreciate these truths of justification.

Because we are dead in sins (Ephesians 2:1), we would never, if left to ourselves, naturally want to trust God. We depend on the Holy Spirit to help us to see our state and need before God, and then to lead us to turn from our sin and put our whole trust in Jesus. We can often get into a mindset of self-pity or remorse, when circumstances seem to pile up on us. It takes the Holy Spirit to turn us from that self-focus to see that our major problem is that of offending God. 'To repent to God' is much more than feeling sorry for ourselves; and 'trust in Jesus' is much more than trying to get a better deal for ourselves. The Holy Spirit is given to bring us to be God-centred in the way we view our sin and why we want to be rid of it. This is the same miraculous work of the Spirit that Peter reported when the gospel made a new breakthrough: 'God has granted even the Gentiles repentance unto life' (Acts 11:18). And so to us as well. That is the Spirit's gift and grace.

What needs to be done from that point on is for us to be changed. John tells us that 'now we are children of

God, and what we will be has not yet been made known' (1 John 3:2). So we are to become more and more like what we are – the children of God. This is the lifelong process of growth, of sanctification. In this process we work together with God to leave our sinful mind and ways behind and to be taken up increasingly with his will and ways.

The Holy Spirit lives in every believer to produce that change. It is only the Spirit who can bring a person to new birth (John 3:6) and to trust in Jesus; and the same Spirit indwells all those he brings to Christ (Romans 8:9). No less a person than 'the Spirit of him who raised Jesus from the dead is living in you' (Romans 8:11). He does not wait until we are perfect or fully surrendered before he takes up residence; if he did, no Christian would have the Spirit. He indwells believers from the very outset of their Christian experience, not because we are good enough, but because we are Christ's and in order to change us. He may be an uncomfortable guest, for sometimes we would rather go along with our sins than with him. But he will not quit on us, and he will complete in the end the good work God has begun (Philippians 1:6). We need to keep on making him welcome, keep on being filled up again and again (Ephesians 5:18), knowing that we are leaky vessels, as D. L. Moody said.

He may sometimes bring us to a crisis in our experience, as some people come to adolescent or mid-life crises. But we will never reach a point in this life where we have 'arrived'. There is no experience on offer from the Holy Spirit which will remove the need constantly to press on for more (Philippians 3:12). A key word in the New Testament is 'renewing'. We are to be 'transformed by the renewing of our mind' (Romans 12:2) and are 'being renewed in knowledge in the image of our Creator' (Colossians 3:10). He is continually refreshing, remoulding, redirecting us – and a lifelong work is not done overnight.

Chiefly the Spirit is working to bring us to increasing likeness to Christ (2 Corinthians 3:18). So what is Christlike? Christlikeness sometimes sounds rather removed from life, rather like haloes and stained glass windows, a state of being unsullied by the world, a detached sanctity, out of contact with others.

Now Christ, self-evidently, is pure and righteous, untainted by sin, with no deceit in his mouth. That said, the most staggering fact about Jesus is that he came down from heaven and he went out to sinners. Christlikeness means following him in such ways. Christ became the friend of tax collectors and sinners (Luke 15:1–2); he spoke of leaving the ninety-nine and going for the one that was lost. Paul said that he was following the example of Christ when he wrote: 'I am not seeking my own good but the good of many, so that they may be saved' (1 Corinthians 10:33). Christlikeness includes growing to become conformed to his image in our character (Romans 8:29), but is radically different from simply cultivating our own spirituality. It was the Pharisees in their righteousness-enclaves who were the furthest removed from likeness to Jesus. So the Spirit works to take us out of our comfort zones and into friendship with people where they are, out there in contact with the culture around us. Jesus left where he was and came to where we are. If we are becoming like Christ, we will do the same, which is why it is linked in our clause with the Spirit's work of 'giving them power for their witness in the world'.

We will probably not feel our need of the Spirit's power too much if we stay in our Christian circles, insulated from those outside. But if we are following Christ and going out to others, to be exposed to their apathy or opposition, to their objections and prejudices, then we will need his power. And it is when we are out there that it is promised to us. It is witnesses going out who will receive his power (Acts 1:8), not those who stay behind in evangelical upper rooms.

We need to understand what 'witness' meant to the first Christians, for 'witness' then had a slightly different meaning. We tend to take it as telling others 'what a difference Christ has made in my life'. There is a place for that. But in Acts witness was much more telling their hearers what a difference Christ had made to the world. The disciples basically pointed to the facts. Peter did not so much say, 'He's my Lord'; they could have dismissed that as the comment of a religious freak. Rather, his witness was to the fact that 'He is *the* Lord'. 'God has made this Jesus, whom you crucified, both Lord and Christ' (Acts 2:36). In other words, he is the Lord of all the universe, of all that is, the one to whom all must bow, the cosmic Christ, a figure you can't avoid, however hard you try. So there was an objective strand – and therefore a strong confidence – in all their witness, as there must be in all true witness today.

Those are the central truths highlighted about what God has done for us and what he is doing in us. These truths explain how grace comes to us, the undeserved and unsought favour of God, and how we can be sure of our acceptance with God. They point out that our relationship depends on Christ's righteousness, not ours; on his settling our debts to God, on his answering for us before God's justice. They explain how we become Christians, as on our knees we thank God the Holy Spirit for having moved us to turn to God to confess our sins and to put our trust in the powerful Saviour. They map out for us the rest of our Christian journey; when we see him, we will be like him (1 John 3:2), but until then we have the resident Holy Spirit to pilot us through and to renew in us the image of God that was so defaced by our sin.

All this is liberating beyond our wildest dreams. If you have ever wrestled inwardly with God about the state of your heart and life, you will be elated to sing the words of this old hymn:

> Before the throne of God above
> I have a strong, a perfect plea:
> For God the just is satisfied
> To look on Christ and pardon me.

The Bible's teaching about our sanctification comes as a huge relief. For one thing, it is so realistic. Those who are justified are still sinners, still liable to doubt and defeat. These truths assure us both that we are accepted, despite being sinners, and that God has put into action his plan to change us. He knows what a job he has taken on and his Spirit in us will keep working with his unfailing energy and will. Nothing about us will deter him or surprise him.

For another thing, this teaching delivers us from thinking that there are any short cuts. Life has very few short cuts of any kind – and most of those that we are offered will short-change us. Learning and growing are, by God's intention, processes. The Bible's basic pictures are of birth, growth, learning and maturing. Such pictures liberate us from any fads and fancies that may fly around the Christian world.

It is futile for us to seek some second crisis experience after conversion which will instantly and miraculously solve all our problems and turn us into perfect followers. What is important is to seek to grow day by day, to go on being filled with the Spirit (Ephesians 5:18) and to love God with all our being.

God may well give us experiences – a second, a third,

a fourth, or a hundred and fourth. Life is experiences with God, each day. The New Testament certainly views our first experience of Christ as revolutionary. What could be more life-changing than the experience of trusting Christ, of being justified, of having eternity settled? It is this that commits us to the whole-life pilgrimage of growing to be like Christ. Growth is generally steady and unspectacular, and the Bible does not encourage us to pin our hopes on some 'get there in one spurt' encounter. So this teaching frees us from a lot of spiritual cul-de-sacs and disappointments, to get on with growing into Christ. As we grow, we will be looking to see that our experiences lead to the fruit of character.

This teaching protects us from the creeping danger of self-righteousness and all spiritual pride. It saves me from thinking that I am or have to be good enough for God. And it sends us out with the revolutionary message of God's free grace. All other religions, whether primitive or modern, sophisticated or philosophical, western or eastern, have one feature in common – they put the initiative with us. They may say to would-be adherents: 'Do! Do what is required – the pilgrimages or the rituals or the good deeds or the sacrifice. It is up to what you do whether you make it to acceptance or heaven.' Or they may say to the enquirer: 'Be! Seek to be what you should be. Engage in meditation or prayers or yoga. It is up to what you are whether you make it to nirvana or reincarnation or whatever you believe in.' Christianity alone says: 'Been and Done!' *Been*, for there is one only who has ever perfectly *been* all that a human being should be. Because of what he alone was, he could bear the sin of others. And *Done!* God has done it. You can't make it. But God is able to receive all who trust him, because he has done all that you couldn't do.

This is the message with which God sends us out, together with the news that he sets about changing those he accepts, so that they can begin to enjoy him and do what pleases him.

Questions

1 Students are often in debt (through no fault of their own!). How does that experience help us to understand justification – God crediting us with righteousness?
2 If justification is God's verdict of the last judgment brought forward to now, how should that affect our security and our motivation?
3 Reflect on what the Bible shows us about Christ; in what areas do we need to grow more like him?
4 Where would we be before God without the Holy Spirit?
5 What is the primary work of the Spirit in believers?
6 What are the implications of the Bible's view of sanctification for our lifelong discipleship?

7

CHRIST'S PEOPLE
AND
CHRIST'S RETURN

What God does for any individual is part of his corporate plan. He is not just in business to redeem individuals and change them. He is out to form a people from every nation, tribe, people and language (Revelation 7:9). Peter wrote to the early Christians, 'Once you were not a people', once you did not belong, you lived as an assortment of individuals, without cohesion or common purpose. But when God called them out of darkness into his wonderful light, God could say that 'now you are a people' (1 Peter 2:9–10).

When we come to God, we come to others as well; we find that we belong to Christ's people. The church of Christ is called by various corporate titles – a people, a priesthood, a nation, a household, a family, a colony. So no confession of Christianity is complete without an affirmation of the one worldwide church: 'The one holy universal church is the Body of Christ to which all true believers belong'.

The church is of paramount importance to every Christian, since it matters so much to God and since all true believers belong to it. No-one can be Christian before God without being incorporated into his church; and that necessarily means involvement with a local church. The clause in the Basis is explicit about the overall nature of the whole people of God, leaving to one side questions about the exact local expressions of the church. There is wisdom in this, for at least two reasons.

One is the obvious fact that people, who equally believe the Bible and fully accept all the truths set out in this Basis, differ in their understanding of how the local and universal aspects of the church should relate. Each denomination has its own slant and few among evangelicals would insist that their views on church issues should have the same rank as our common views, say, on the atonement. So there is a proper reserve among Bible believers about riding their particular views of the church too hard. The issues may be important for Christian witness – after all, in order to function in practice a church must decide whether or not to have bishops or elders, infant or believers' baptism, etc. But these issues do not come within the 'fundamental truths' of Christianity.

Silence in a Basis about the local church is not a sign that it is thought unimportant. Rather, it is an invitation to evangelicals to work out their views, as they are persuaded in their own minds, and also in charity with those who differ on matters such as baptism, church order or practice.

A second reason for concentrating on the overall concept of the church is that, in most places, we face a situation quite unlike that of the New Testament. Take first-century Ephesus as an example. We do not know exactly how the church was structured there. Was there a building where they could all meet publicly? Almost certainly not. Were the elders there actually over the various houses (house churches?) where believers met (Acts 20:20)? Probably. Whatever the structure, there was a unified people of God in Ephesus, with no denominations holding separate or rival services. Today, look at any town: all the congregations wear a denominational label (even the newer 'unde-nominational' ones). None of them can properly claim to be in the same position in their town as the congregation or house churches in Ephesus – or, if they do, they unchurch all the others. All are marked by some additional, other-than-gospel label.

The church at Ephesus did not need any other body to help it reach students; it could have sent its appropriate members to the local university campus genuinely to represent Christianity. Any congregation today that attempts the same is liable to be seen as representing the Presbyterians or Anglicans, the Baptists or Methodists, the Pentecostals or charismatics. Hence the appropriateness of Christian Unions or student groups on campus, since they can set aside these differences and seek to represent plain, Bible Christianity and its core truths. The same principle applies in other areas of Christian work, where societies or agencies with limited objectives are sent by the churches for particular tasks.

Christian Unions are not churches or substitute churches; they lack many of the normal marks of the church. They do not usually have regular biblical ministry from their own membership; they do not initiate people into the church through baptism, or feed people regularly at the Lord's Table. They seldom exercise discipline and obviously do not have the range of ages and backgrounds that a local church would. But they are a missionary force of the whole church on campus. Their members are members of local churches. Christian Unions receive their members from the churches and send them back into the churches. Christian students are simply the people best placed to reach their peers. They study, live, eat, think, talk and mix with other students in a way that is totally natural and not open to non-students. They relate to other students as friends and Christians, not as people wearing outside labels, denominational or other.

The interdenominational nature of a student group is

a strong biblical plus in its witness; it does not have to defend or put in front of non-Christians a set of lesser distinctives; it can simply be there for the gospel, no more and no less. Many churches, of course, are gospel-centred rather than primarily expressing a denominational ethos.

There is therefore no conflict between the roles of church and CU; rather the reverse. A wise church will encourage student groups to get on with their on-campus witness without control or interference; a wise CU will value the counsel and support of understanding local churches.

Relationships vary from time to time, but the best relationship probably includes these two factors:

1. CU members regularly attending a local church and being welcomed there, both to its Sunday services and into the homes of church members. Churches can have a great influence for good, in pastoral and evangelistic ways, with the wisdom God has given them.

2. Churches encouraging students to make their mark for God on campus, rather than drawing them away from the student scene into the full round of church activities. It is a great temptation to churches to use the enthusiasm of students, but the opportunities of student years can never be recaptured and need to be taken at the time.

The clause highlights the basic truths about the church that are not in dispute. The church is one: not a collection of separate 'churches', but one body of those who have been redeemed by the blood of Christ. This oneness should transcend all sectional loyalties.

The church is holy, but not in the sense of being perfect. The New Testament had to call on Christians frequently to leave their sins, gossip, slander and feuds. But the church is holy in the sense that its members are called to holiness and have been set apart to live for God.

The church is universal or worldwide, reaching to and including people from every social, economic, educational, cultural and ethnic background. It brings its message into the culture of every people, wanting them each (as we see from Acts 2:6, 8 and 11) to hear of God and express their response in their own local dialect. The church across the globe does not have to conform to one ritual or pattern, but can express the same basic love to God in its own local way – indeed, it is imperative that it does so. A church that exhibits an imported culture is a liability to God. Paul wrote to the Christians at Rome, among other things, to steer them away from being either dominated by Jewishness or set against Jews. The one way would have alienated Gentiles, the other would have offended Jews, and Paul wanted a church where Jews and Gentiles all accepted each other as Christ had accepted them (Romans 15:7). The church at the heart of the empire needed to exhibit Christ, not factions; only in that way could it be seen as the 'dwelling in which God lives by his Spirit' (Ephesians 2:21–22).

The church is the body of Christ, meaning that it belongs to him, that he is its head (Ephesians 4:15), and that it is only to take final instructions from him. No human can rule the church since that is for Christ alone, through his authoritative word. Christ is not merely the theoretical or titular head of the church, but its active and actual head. It is the gifts, openings and challenges that he has given to any congregation or assembly that should in practice determine what that church does rather than the slots that people think need to be filled.

Being a body means that all its members have complementary functions, and the gifts to fulfil them, by which they contribute to building each other up. This sense of belonging to and needing each other is foreign to rugged, western individualism, but very much part of God's plan and a foretaste of heaven.

Interestingly, the chief reason made explicit in the New Testament for Christians to meet together is not to worship God, though we will naturally want to do that on those occasions when we meet, and in the rest of our lives. The explicit reason given is that we should 'encourage one another', 'spur one another on towards love and good deeds' (Hebrews 10:24–25). 'When you come together, all … must be done for the strengthening of the church' (1 Corinthians 14:26). The aim is that we build each other up. That is why we need each other and why we must meet others, not merely be in the same building with them for a service.

These truths explain that God's church is bigger than our perspective and experience of it. They imply that all Christians should be committed to the church and its local expression, working in it and through it for God. Students who win students for Christ, as the CU fulfils its particular mission role, will want them to be integrated quickly with a congregation. CUs are part of the whole church's ministry, not vice versa.

These truths liberate us from getting hung up too much about denominations or divisions, in order to focus on expressing our God-given oneness with all who honour his Son and make his gospel known. These truths put disputed church matters into perspective.

These truths protect us from falling for any claims to have the exclusive truth about the church, or from any who may try to take over a student group for sectional teaching that does not keep the central truths central. The church needs to be preserved from secondary squabbles, since its main battle is for the minds and hearts of people who are at the moment outside its membership and in darkness.

And the thought of the church sends us out to bring more people in, as Christ builds his church by continually adding new converts to it.

The thrust of God's truth in general, and of the purpose of the church in particular, is to enthuse us about and give us vision for winning the world for Christ. World mission beckons. The church is a going-out body, always following Christ as he seeks and saves the lost.

And so to the last things: 'The Lord Jesus will return in person, to judge everyone, to execute God's just condemnation on those who have not repented and to receive the redeemed to eternal glory'. The final clause of the confession brings us to the end, the conclusion of what will happen in time and the start of what we will experience in eternity. This puts Christians in a uniquely favoured position. We know where we are coming from – God's creation; we know where we are going and how it will all end. This gives us a confident hope that puts our present life into perspective.

The chief fact that this highlights is that God has a plan for all history, that he is working it out as year succeeds year, and that he will personally bring his plan to his conclusion. Curiosity about the end rises in all of us. What lies beyond death? Now that we have the capacity to destroy this world (a scenario that no previous generation has had to face), many people are anxious to know how will it all finish.

This clause underlines the Bible's consistent teaching that the present stage of history, between the two comings of Christ, will end. The universe will not run on in a steadily evolving way, getting ever better and better. It is now 'groaning … as we wait for the redemption of our bodies' (Romans 8:22–23). It will finish, both because it is so riddled with the effects of sin, and because God has something better – the new heaven and the new earth (Revelation 21:1–2).

This present 'order of things' (Revelation 21:4) will finish on the day long ago decreed by God. Even the incarnate Son of God on earth did not know the date, but his Father does (Mark 13:32). The end of time is in his timing. God's Son will return in person in great power and glory. He will return as he went (Acts 1:11), dramatically and visibly.

Some Christians down the years have been quick to speculate about the details of Christ's return or to offer their interpretations to explain the order of events. On the whole, the more details these predictions have provided, the less conviction they have carried. Scripture concentrates on the main fact and on its spiritual and moral implications for our lives.

Christ's return will be the end of any opportunity for people to respond to the gospel, because the return will usher in the final judgment, where all must appear before the judge (2 Corinthians 5:10). The parable of the ten virgins has a solemn phrase: 'And the door was shut' to the latecomers (Matthew 25:10–12).

The fact that Christ will judge everyone, every man and woman, is entirely fitting in relation to who Christ is (the Lord of the universe), but entirely unpalatable to contemporary thought. Judgment is a redundant and repugnant category in a relativistic age, but the Bible teaches it – and it makes sense. The Christian world-view recognizes that this life has plenty of injustice, but that one day justice will prevail, wrongs will be righted, good will triumph and evil will be destroyed. Many people spend their lives demanding justice from God: they will get it, because it is God's nature to act justly.

The basis of judgment was brought out in the earlier clause on human nature: it will be according to a person's light. Every person has access to some awareness of God from the created order – to the fact that God exists and that he has eternal power (Romans 1:18–20). 'What may be known about God is plain to them, so that men are without excuse'. Those who have rejected the light available to them will be accountable for that.

In fact, faced with this 'general revelation' of God, Paul says that people actually suppress the truth and are culpable for doing so. It is wickedness rather than ignorance that leads them to do this. Far from all routes leading to God, that passage in Romans 1 suggests that it is more a case of all routes leading away from God. These truths have aspects that are sobering, but they are as clear in the Bible as all the other basic truths.

Those who refuse to come to a right attitude to God will suffer God's just condemnation. The judge of all the earth will do right (Genesis 18:25). 'He will punish those who do not know God and do not obey the gospel of our Lord Jesus. They will be punished with everlasting destruction and shut out from the presence of the Lord' (2 Thessalonians 1:8–9).

The redeemed will have another destiny: they will be received into eternal glory. Heaven waits! They will be welcomed into the eternal home, to keep company with their God – Father, Son and Spirit – and all their brothers and sisters. They will know him as all the while he has known them (1 Corinthians 13:12). They will see, whereas previously they had to trust (1 John 3:2). They will be satisfied, whereas before they had to hope. The new order of thing will be ushered in, with an end to death, mourning, crying and pain (Revelation 21:4). That verse implies that now, in this life, we are in the 'old order of things', where these sad experiences occur. There is no promise of their final removal here – but they will not be present in glory. No wonder that we want to cry with John: 'Amen. (So be it.) Come, Lord Jesus' (Revelation 22:20).

This final clause, awesome but uplifting, explains what God's final curtain will reveal. The world will not end with a human finger on the button. Jesus will return, the Master who went on his journey will come back

(John 14:3). We will meet him and be with him for ever, in the company of the redeemed (1 Thessalonians 4:17).

This truth liberates us to lift up our heads to the coming king. We are released from anxious care about the future. All will end well, the last scene will put everything right. If death should come before then, it cannot separate us from the love of God (Romans 8:38–39).

This truth protects us from all kinds of fears; our hearts do not need to be troubled, for we trust in God (John 14:1). This truth also preserves us from apathy about those who do not know Christ, the lost. They are lost, as we were. They need to hear, now, in this time of opportunity, before it is too late.

Finally, therefore, this truth sends us out for Christ, so that we may meet him not with shame, but with pure joy. 'You ought to live holy and godly lives as you look forward to the day of God and speed its coming … since you are looking forward to this, make every effort to be found spotless, blameless and at peace with him' (2 Peter 3:11–14).

Questions

1 How does God reveal the value he sets on his church?
2 Churches, composed of the likes of us, are never perfect. How can we contribute to their growth?
3 What is the most important Christian response to the certainty of Christ's return?
4 What sense of hope is there in society around us? How can we speak of true hope?
5 Then 'There will be no more death or mourning or crying or pain, for the old order of things has passed away' (Revelation 21:4). Then, not yet. What can we expect while the old order is still with us?

8

THE BASIS
IN THE LIFE OF
A STUDENT GROUP

The Doctrinal Basis expresses and provides a foundation for unity, for Christian union – and therefore for evangelical student groups or Christian Unions. It focuses on essentials and so helps to minimize or eliminate division.

What should a group do when a divisive issue arises? Sometimes the answer is to say to both parties: 'Yes, we do differ on this issue and we may not be able to resolve the differences. But maybe we can agree on two things: first, that the matters on which we disagree are not as important as the gospel itself; and second, that our energies are much better spent on our united battle for the minds and hearts of unbelieving students than on battling with each other.' The Doctrinal Basis helps to keep the essential convictions to the fore, so that we focus on evangelism.

The Basis also helps to guide and guard the leadership of a student group or CU. It can help to steer it away from actual errors or from cul-de-sacs or diversions. It is a marker set down on our way, a signpost to the path of truth along which God's witnesses have walked in every century. It is not formality or constitution-mindedness that moves a Christian group to ask their leaders wholeheartedly and thoughtfully to affirm that these are their convictions too. It is the desire to hand on the baton of faith to reliable men and women (2 Timothy 2:2).

How can a student group use the Basis?

For Christians

We assume that the group has regular teaching meetings. We also assume that their aim is to give the best possible coverage of Bible truth in each individual's (three?) student years. In those circumstances the Basis can be a regular ingredient in such ways as these:

(i) The weekly teaching meeting could take one or two clauses per week, to fit in with the length of term or semester; or

(ii) one meeting each term could take a clause of the Basis, aiming in that way to cover the Basis in three years.

These meetings could take an overview of the Bible's treatment of each doctrine, as in this book; or could find one passage of the Bible relating to each truth and open that up.

When so many Christians mistakenly assume the three 'Ds' (that Doctrine is Dry and Dull), the approach to such meetings is crucial. It may help to use three questions – why, what and how?

(a) Why is the chosen doctrine important? This is the question of relevance. The Bible handles truths in a way that constantly relates them to life. So it is worth showing at the outset of any talk the particular aspects of the Christian life to which the truth relates. All these convictions have a practical bearing on, for example, our ideas of God (and so our devotion), our praying or assurance, our evangelism or message, our obedience or temptations. All of them stand in some contrast to views of God, Jesus, human nature, community, hope, etc. that are current in society. If we bring out these connections, Christians will quickly see the relevance of truth.

(b) What does the Bible teach in the doctrine? The speaker (or group leader) will need to study to bring out a clear statement of what the Bible says – not what the speaker thinks or what the hearers prefer, but what the Bible says. (We do not believe the Bible's truths because they are all congenial, but because they happen to be true.) If a student group is having to prepare its own talk or study, the suggested books (p. 95) will be a great help.

(c) How does this truth affect our lives? An abstract talk on doctrine will probably not be very biblical, because the Bible always challenges us with truth, to teach, rebuke, correct and train in righteousness (2 Timothy 3:16). Often such a meeting will appropriately close with a time of thanksgiving for what God has revealed, and of prayer for grace to live it out.

For non-Christians

The Doctrinal Basis for non-Christians? No and yes. No, in that none would argue for starting evangelism by thrusting the Basis at an unbeliever. But yes, in that the truths of the Basis all have an evangelistic force. It is quite possible and appropriate to take the central thrust of each clause and turn it into an evangelistic or apologetic theme. The clauses could be used like this, though these are only examples:

(a) There are many pressures today for a multi-faith approach, in the belief that all religions are equally valid, that pluralism is the right stance. So a meeting on 'only one God' could challenge the basis of other beliefs and present the God of the Bible.

(b) 'Why does God allow …?' is often asked. Behind that is the question of 'who is in control – of the world in general, or your individual life?' Is life led by fate or chance or evolution? The sovereignty of God comes in here.

(c) As James Sire puts it: 'Why should we believe anything at all?' In what do people ground their beliefs – for beliefs they all have? Is there one voice to which we should all listen? Has God spoken? The Bible comes in here – perhaps the evidence for the Gospels' accounts.

(d) Everybody observes and suffers from human nature. What is wrong with the world? Do the secular explanations stand up? How to explain conscience? What the Bible says on people is right up to date, uniquely able to explain what everyone experiences.

(e) Always sharply relevant is the person and life of Jesus. Was he mad, bad or God? What claims did he make? How to explain the resurrection?

(f) What is the answer to the human condition? How can people cope with failings, frustration, hopelessness? Are we driven to despair, the logical end of a godless outlook? Can anyone help? What is the connection between all this and why Christ died?

(g) Is it possible to have a new start, the slate wiped clean? Can a guilty conscience find rest? What can be done about the sense of accountability that we cannot totally escape? Justification speaks here.

(h) Many feel trapped not only by their external circumstances, but also by their inner drives and pressures. Can anyone get them out? The work of the Holy Spirit is vital.

(i) Once delivered, how will they then live? Where can the power come from to live for God, to follow Christ, to do good rather than evil? From the indwelling Holy Spirit.

(j) Many people feel essentially alone in life, with no sense of being part of any meaningful group. They feel alienated and lonely in the midst of hundreds of fellow students. The church speaks of belonging to and being valued and loved by others, as all are loved by God.

(k) How will things end? For the individual, for society, for the world? What is the future? What about death and after? Christ's return has a clear evangelistic thrust of challenge and hope.

Many other evangelistic or apologetic themes will come to mind, but these are enough to show that the truths in the Basis have an application to evangelism, as well as to building Christians up in the faith.

Maybe the teaching meeting for Christians and the evangelistic meeting could be related, so that the one becomes preparation and training for the other – or follow-up to it. Why not devote a session of your student group's committee to discussing these possibilities before you plan the programme?

9

THE BASIS IN THE LIGHT OF ONGOING DEBATE

Dogmatism? No thanks

Some people are dogmatic about everything; we all know a few like that. Curiously, however, everybody is dogmatic about something. That is true even today, even in an era when dogmatism is widely taken as the sign of the fringe fanatic.

We live in the age of tolerance and the open society. Many beliefs exist within our communities – religious, non-religious and anti-religious. This pluralism is a fact and we must welcome living with it, in the name of religious liberty for all. People must have freedom to consider other views, weigh the evidence and, if persuaded, change their beliefs and practise them unimpeded. Often, however, pluralism is turned into an article of faith, an anti-dogmatic faith that holds that all views, religious or non-religious, are equally valid and that no-one must claim otherwise.

This brings out one of the inner contradictions of our age. Everything is relative. There are no absolutes and it is impossible to find any perspective which will yield a coherent overview of life. We cannot work from any sacred book, since nothing any author has written has any objective sense. We cannot learn from history, for that has no discernible meaning either. All that on the one hand, with the logical consequence that there is no 'capital T' truth and that each person can only try to find some personal 'small t' truth for him or herself.

On the other hand, dogmatism persists and grows, even if it is only in the claim that you absolutely cannot be dogmatic about anything. Ride relativism hard enough and it becomes an absolute assertion: 'There are no absolutes'. In other words, everyone sooner or later comes to a crunch point where they take an absolute stance. Relativism cannot even sustain itself and, logically, ultimately self-destructs.

This dilemma can be seen in the outworking of relativism's passionate belief in tolerance. All views must be allowed space, all religions have the same validity, all philosophies must be heard. We may not and must not judge between them if there are people who wish to follow them. Every belief-system must be tolerated, except the one that claims that it alone is right. Relativism can turn out to be extremely intolerant of Christianity. The claim that Jesus is the only way to God is offensive.

The assertion that certain life styles are wrong before God, that (for example) homosexual practice and Christian discipleship are incompatible, causes outrage. Exclusive claims are intolerable; relativism draws a line in the sand after all. A national newspaper article can sweepingly denounce the dogmatism of a student Christian Union (which believed that people were either saved or lost), but the writer is never called on to defend his dogmatism – because he, after all, believes in 'tolerance'. It is a case of anything or nothing, but not something. Tolerance allows us to have any belief or no belief, but obviously does not like us to have definite belief. Then it becomes dogmatic.

No wonder, then, that such dogmatism leads to clashes of views over the nature of Christianity and its truth claims. Many of these clashes are variations on one theme – the relationship of truth (or truth claims) to freedom. It is here that Christians most radically differ from others. Christians believe the words of Jesus, when he said, in reference to his own teaching: 'You will know the truth, and the truth will set you free' (John 8:32). The truth, according to Jesus, does not put blinkers over our minds, restrict our vision or cramp our lives. It sets us free, saying: 'Get hold of what is authentic and you will find true liberty'. It gives us the spiritual health to enjoy that freedom. Truth includes what the New Testament calls 'sound' teaching. 'Sound doctrine' (Titus 1:9; 2:1) means health-promoting instruction that encourages spiritual fitness and frees us to live full lives before God. There is no freedom apart from the truth. To be free, we need to begin with what God has revealed.

The opposite view, espoused with equal firmness, turns Jesus' saying around. In effect, it says: 'You must seek freedom and that freedom will make your life authentic and true. Break away from truth claims, it argues, cast off the chains of dogma, be free; stop thinking that there is any overarching explanation to life; and then you will find your authentic existence, your own true self, your personal fulfilment and reality for you.'

We can see this clash of views around us in society. It does not often present itself overtly in exactly those terms. It has sometimes been veiled behind smoke-screen talk of being new, modern or progressive rather than traditional, out-of-date or reactionary. The issue has been buried under an avalanche of words like obstructionist, fundamentalist, anti-intellectual, etc. Now it is most likely to be hidden behind denials of the existence of any single source of truth or meaning.

Ironically, then, dogmatism refuses to lie down and die. Even though the whole climate of our age, in pop culture as in academic circles, proclaims that none can make universal claims because everything is relative, people persist in making such assertive generalizations. Maybe this is because of the way we are (the way God made us?). In view of everyone being prone to some dogmatism, the Christian will want to ask: what is the basis of any dogmatism? He or she will want to answer: God and his revelation, both in the Bible and in his Son, the living Lord. There is ample evidence for that answer. Other answers are subjective and lack such evidence. Christians can properly challenge others about their basis. In the end, if God has spoken, we have enough to build on. What he says is a matter of truth, not opinion.

Why have a Basis?

As we have seen, people argue today against having any clear statement of belief at all. Some object on theological grounds. It is said to be too exclusive in its truth claims, too narrow in its outlook, and too rigid in its application. Such comments generally come from a theological stance that dislikes absolute affirmations and is much keener on an open-ended approach. The starting point, rather than the evidence, determines the outcome.

What we have seen is that the truths in the Basis come clearly from Scripture; we may or may not find them congenial, but they are there – and together they form an objectively-based and coherent world-view.

Some object on academic grounds. They say that a strong confessional statement is incompatible with an academic institution like a university, which ought to instill a proper scepticism into its students. Surely, however, minds are like mouths in this respect: meant to open only to close on something solid. Academic enquiry is not opposed to definite conclusions, provided that they are well-grounded. As Martin Luther said, 'The Holy Spirit is no sceptic', so why should we be? And as Harry Blamires pointed out, it may be humbler to accept God's revealed definites than to hold on to our 'open-minded' indefinites, in the presumptuous belief that one day we will get ourselves to the truth without God's help.

Other objections spring from psychological theory – that people pass through a phase in which they tend to conform and to seek the security of a defined group. To such people, of the student age-range, a Doctrinal Basis is attractive. It gives them an identity and a sense of certainty. The argument is that the Basis is a crutch, a psychological security token; needing a basis is a stage through which people will pass. Nice theory and full marks for ingenuity, but not so hot on the evidence. It may well be true that some people look for such a crutch; a Christian Union has all sorts in it and welcomes them all. But people of all ages, down all the centuries of history, including some of the most able intellectuals and stable personalities of their generations, have held to such confessions. They are by no means the preserve only of insecure adolescents. And such a theory neglects the fact that many people come to such convictions from having been very secure in their atheism or opposition. They were not 'seeking security'; they just happened to find that the Bible was true! Then the sense of security followed.

Some object to a Doctrinal Basis on the ground that those who hold to such convictions tend to shy away from cooperating with those who hold conflicting or vague views. But if they hold back, it is only because they believe truth is vital. People's eternities depend on the core truths of the gospel, and it is unloving and misleading to engage in cooperation that would muddy the waters on those issues. We have to decide whose voice we will heed. If God has spoken, we can but follow.

If we are invited to join, say, a mission which will include views which do not seem biblical, how should we respond? We need to think carefully. First, we need to ascertain what those views are and, centrally, what place they give to Christ's atonement on the cross. Then we need to know what tests to apply. To Paul the test was: what will make the gospel clear? This was the thrust of his argument in Galatians 1:6–9. It was the same with Jesus: if it is the truth that sets people free (John 8:32), what will make the truth clear? It is obviously good to have many people doing this, but the basic question is not 'Can we all get together?', but 'What will avoid confusion and clarify the biblical gospel?' A Doctrinal Basis is a summary statement of what we are privileged to proclaim to a confused and dying world.

Christians are called to 'keep the faith once delivered to the saints'; such a Doctrinal Basis is simply a way of affirming that faith today. In this atmosphere it is an amazing honour to make known the great revealed truths. Christians down the ages have had to make plain what the Bible teaches and to express that in creeds and other statements. They have counted it a privilege to do so, to be stewards of God's truth.

How a Basis arises

Confessional statements can be, and have been down history, put together in a variety of ways. Some of them, for example, start with God as the ultimate being and then move on to how he has revealed himself (as in the UCCF statement); others speak first of the Bible as the source of our knowledge of God and then move on to what it says about him. These differences of order are generally of small consequence.

All summaries of Christian belief are a balance between the unchanging truths of God on the one hand, and the pressing circumstances at the time of their compilation on the other. Most of the great creeds (like many of the New Testament letters) were drawn up to combat particular errors. The letter to the Galatians counters those who wanted to add something (circumcision) to what Christ had done as a condition of salvation. Colossians counters those who claimed that they alone had the secret knowledge necessary for salvation. We do not ditch these letters because they come out of a particular historical, geographical, sociological or religious context.

Some of the early creeds set out to confound views which misled people about Christ's person. The confessions of the great Reformation period set out the freshness of God's justification of sinners against the background of a 'we must earn it' religion.

The UCCF or IFES Basis is no different in respect to this balance. The prevailing theological trend of the last hundred years or more up to the present time is to deny the supernatural, to debunk the Bible as being (not just containing) the Word of God, and to decry the 'Christ in our place' view of the cross.

All the classic creeds and confessions that set out the biblical faith thus have some marks of their origins, but remain true. Fresh heresies may arise and need to be confronted – but few heresies are totally fresh. Often the older statements clearly contain or imply the truths needed now to refute current errors (is there anything new under the sun?). At other times there may be reason to add or replace a clause. It could be argued that a Basis for today should unpack more of the biblical view of creation in an environment-conscious society; or that it should say more on the church, at a time when we are becoming more aware of the dangers of western individualism; that it should talk about the role of the Christian in society and how evangelism relates to social action.

All these are important truths, but should they be in a Basis? It is, after all, only a Basis, not a commentary or explanation of all the implications of those beliefs. It is not an exhaustive statement since it claims only that the fundamental truths of Christianity *include* the clauses that follow. Some truths are not included in the Basis because Christians, who equally hold to the core truths, differ on them – baptism and church government are obvious examples. Others are not touched on because they only surface from time to time, perhaps according to whatever is a contemporary issue at a given period.

So we can take it enthusiastically for what it is, no more and no less. The Bible, the Word of God, comes to us in words and propositions in many literary forms – story, poetry, allegory, argument, etc. The Basis simply tries to précis the message and thrust of the Bible and, as a summary, helps us to articulate what the Bible teaches.

It is obviously not infallible as is the Bible; it is always to be tested by what the Bible says. It is subordinate to the Bible. Yet it also comes to us in the great, continuous stream of biblical confessions expressing the faith of God's people down the running centuries. It is not an aberration, not a sectarian side-show, but in the central flow of historic Christian belief. It comes with the weight of that good tradition behind it. In that sense it is also incidentally a statement about the importance of the church, as it expresses the faith of God's one people from the New Testament. It does not put forward the views of a few individuals, but of the company of those who have run the race before us and have now entered their rest. To be unfair to Martin Luther's words, it is not so much an affirmation of 'Here I stand' as 'here *we* stand'. It enshrines the corporate, humble, accepted wisdom of God's people down the years.

Postscript

In these pages we have tried to explore and expound the main truths of the Bible. We have done so in the spirit of the Scots Confession, drawn up in 1560 by John Knox and five other Scottish Reformers. The language is quaintly dated, but the meaning is clear.

> The doctrine taught in our kirks is contained in the written word of God, to wit, in the Books of the Old and New Testaments … If any man will note in this our confession any article or sentence repugnant to God's holy word, that it would please him of his gentleness, and for Christian charities' sake, to admonish us of the same in writing; and we upon our honour and fidelity, by God's grace, do promise unto him satisfaction from the mouth of God, that is from His Holy Scriptures, or else reformation of that which shall prove to be amiss.

FOR FURTHER READING

Know the Truth by Bruce J. Milne (IVP)

Concise Theology by James I. Packer (IVP)

Systematic Theology by Wayne Grudem (IVP)

God's Words by James I. Packer (IVP)

Discovering Christianity by Richard Cunningham (UCCF)

The Bible Speaks Today (IVP) is a series of expositions of Bible books that would be an excellent basis for study of particular passages on doctrinal themes.